Religions
of the
World

Without freedom of religion

Many people live in countries where religious freedom is restricted or prohibited. An annual report by the U.S. Department of State classifies the policies and actions of those nations into five categories.

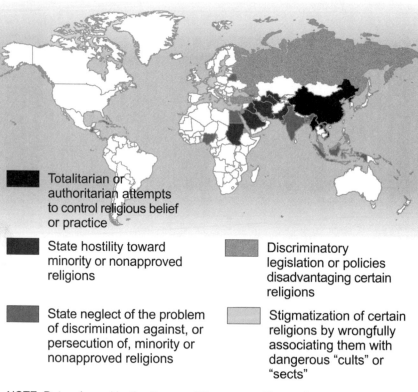

Totalitarian or authoritarian attempts to control religious belief or practice

State hostility toward minority or nonapproved religions

Discriminatory legislation or policies disadvantaging certain religions

State neglect of the problem of discrimination against, or persecution of, minority or nonapproved religions

Stigmatization of certain religions by wrongfully associating them with dangerous "cults" or "sects"

NOTE: Data released by the Bureau of Democracy, Human Rights, and Labor on Oct. 7, 2002

SOURCE: U.S. Department of State

AP

RELIGIONS
OF THE
WORLD

NEW RELIGIONS

Carol S. Matthews
Associate Adjunct Professor
of History and Humanities,
Johnson County Community College

Series Consulting Editor Ann Marie B. Bahr
Professor of Religious Studies,
South Dakota State University

Foreword by Martin E. Marty
Professor Emeritus,
University of Chicago Divinity School

CHELSEA HOUSE
PUBLISHERS
A Haights Cross Communications ⌁ Company ®
Philadelphia

COVER   The Church of Jesus Christ of Latter-day Saints temple, San Diego, California.

FRONTIS   Throughout the world, freedom of religion is generally regarded as a basic human right. However, there are still countries that restrict or prohibit religious practice. Shown here is a U.S. Department of State graphic that highlights countries that still prohibit or restrict freedom of religion.

CHELSEA HOUSE PUBLISHERS

VP, NEW PRODUCT DEVELOPMENT   Sally Cheney
DIRECTOR OF PRODUCTION   Kim Shinners
CREATIVE MANAGER   Takeshi Takahashi
MANUFACTURING MANAGER   Diann Grasse

Staff for NEW RELIGIONS

EXECUTIVE EDITOR   Lee Marcott
EDITOR   Christian Green
PRODUCTION EDITOR   Noelle Nardone
PHOTO EDITOR   Sarah Bloom
SERIES AND COVER DESIGNER   Keith Trego
LAYOUT   21st Century Publishing and Communications, Inc.

A Haights Cross Communications ✦ Company ®

www.chelseahouse.com

First Printing

9 8 7 6 5 4 3 2 1

Library of Congress Cataloging-in-Publication Data

Matthews, Carol S., 1961–
    New religions/Carol S. Matthews.
        p. cm.—(Religions of the world)
    Includes bibliographical references.
    ISBN 0-7910-8096-X (hardcover)
    1. Cults—Juvenile literature. 2. Sects—Juvenile literature. I. Title. II. Series.
BP603.M32 2005
200'.9'034—dc22

                                                      2004024514

All links and web addresses were checked and verified to be correct at the time of publication. Because of the dynamic nature of the web, some addresses and links may have changed since publication and may no longer be valid.

CONTENTS

Foreword

Martin E. Marty

On this very day, like all other days, hundreds of millions of people around the world will turn to religion for various purposes.

On the one hand, there are purposes that believers in any or all faiths, as well as unbelievers, might regard as positive and benign. People turn to religion or, better, to their own particular faith, for the experience of healing and to inspire acts of peacemaking. They want to make sense of a world that can all too easily overwhelm them because it so often seems to be meaningless and even absurd. Religion then provides them with beauty, inspires their souls, and impels them to engage in acts of justice and mercy.

To be informed citizens of our world, readers have good reason to learn about these features of religions that mean so much to so many. Those who study the faiths do not have to agree with any of them and could not agree with all of them, different as they are. But they need basic knowledge of religions to understand other people and to work out strategies for living with them.

On the other hand—and religions always have an "other hand"—believers in any of the faiths, and even unbelievers who are against all of them, will find their fellow humans turning to their religions for purposes that seem to contradict all those positive features. Just as religious people can heal and be healed, they can also kill or be killed in the name of faith. So it has been through history.

This killing can be literal: Most armed conflicts and much terrorism today are inspired by the stories, commands, and promises that come along with various faiths. People can and do read and act upon scriptures that can breed prejudice and that lead them to reject other beliefs and believers. Or the killing can be figurative, which means that faiths can be deadening to the spirit. In the name of faith, many people are repressed, oppressed, sometimes victimized and abused.

If religion can be dangerous and if it may then come with "Handle with Care" labels, people who care for their own security, who want to lessen tensions and inspire concord, have to equip themselves by learning something about the scriptures and stories of their own and other faiths. And if they simply want to take delight in human varieties and imaginings, they will find plenty to please them in lively and reliable accounts of faiths.

A glance at television or at newspapers and magazines on almost any day will reveal stories that display one or both sides of religion. However, these stories usually have to share space with so many competing accounts, for example, of sports and entertainment or business and science, that writers and broadcasters can rarely provide background while writing headlines. Without such background, it is hard to make informed judgments.

The series RELIGIONS OF THE WORLD is designed to provide not only background but also rich illustrative material about the foreground, presenting the many features of faiths that are close at hand. Whoever reads all the volumes in the series will find that these religions have some elements in common. Overall, one can deduce that their followers take certain things with ultimate seriousness: human dignity, devotion to the sacred, the impulse to live a moral life. Yet few people are inspired by religions in general. They draw strength from what they hold particularly. These particulars of each faith are not always contradictory to those of others, but they are different in important ways. It is simply a fact that believers are informed and inspired by stories told in separate and special ways.

A picture might make all this vivid: Reading about a religion, visiting a place of worship, or coming into the company of those who believe in and belong to a particular faith, is like entering a room. Religions are, in a sense, spiritual "furnished apartments." Their adherents have placed certain pictures on the wall and moved in with their own kind of furnishings, having developed their special ways of receiving or blocking out light from such places. Some of their figurative apartments are airy, and some stress strength and security.

Philosopher George Santayana once wrote that, just as we do not speak language, we speak particular languages, so we have religion not as a whole but as religions "in particular." The power of each living and healthy religion, he added, consists in "its special and surprising message and in the bias which that revelation gives to life." Each creates "another world to live in."

The volumes in this series are introductions to several spiritual furnished apartments, guides to the special and surprising messages of these large and complex communities of faith, or religions. These are not presented as a set of items in a cafeteria line down which samplers walk, tasting this, rejecting that, and moving on. They are not bids for window-shoppers or shoppers of any sort, though it may be that a person without faith might be drawn to one or another expression of the religions here described. The real intention of the series is to educate.

Education could be dull and drab. Picture a boring professor standing in front of a class and droning on about distant realities. The authors in this series, however, were chosen because they can bring readers up close to faiths and, sometimes better, to people of faith; not to religion but to people who are religious in particular ways.

As one walks the streets of a great metropolis, it is not easy and may not even be possible to deduce the faith-commitments of those one passes unless they wear a particular costume—some garb or symbol prescribed by their faith. Therefore, while passing them by, it is not likely that one can learn much about the dreams and hopes, the fears and intentions, of those around them.

These books, in effect, stop the procession of passersby and bid visitors to enter those sanctuaries where communities worship. Each book could serve as a guide to worship. Several years ago, a book called *How to Be a Perfect Stranger* offered brief counsel on how to feel and to be at home among worshipers from other traditions. This series recognizes that we are not strangers to each other only in sanctuaries. We carry over our attachments to conflicting faiths where we go to work or vote or serve in the military or have fun. These "carryovers" tend to come from the basic stories and messages of the several faiths.

The publishers have taken great pains to assign their work to authors of a particular sort. Had these been anti-religious or anti–the religion about which they write, they would have done a disservice. They would, in effect, have been blocking the figurative doors to the faiths or smashing the furniture in the sanctuaries. On the other hand, it would be wearying and distorting had the assignment gone to public relations agents, advertisers who felt called to claim "We're Number One!" concerning the faith about which they write.

Fair-mindedness and accuracy are the two main marks of these authors. In rather short compass, they reach a wide range of subjects, focusing on everything one needs to advance basic understanding. Their books are like mini-encyclopedias, full of information. They introduce the holidays that draw some neighbors to be absent from work or school for a day or a season. They include galleries of notable figures in each faith-community.

Since most religions in the course of history develop different ways in the many diverse places where they thrive, or because they attract intelligent, strong-willed leaders and writers, they come up with different emphases. They divide and split off into numberless smaller groups: Protestant and Catholic and Orthodox Christians, Shiite and Sunni Muslims, Orthodox and Reform Jews, and many kinds of Buddhists and Hindus. The writers in this series do justice to these variations, providing a kind of map without which one will get lost in the effort to understand.

Some years ago, a rabbi friend, Samuel Sandmel, wrote a book about his faith called *The Enjoyment of Scripture*. What an astonishing concept, some might think: After all, religious scriptures deal with desperately urgent, life-and-death-and-eternity issues. They have to be grim and those who read them likewise. Not so. Sandmel knew what the authors of this series also know and impart: The journeys of faith and the encounter with the religions of others include pleasing and challenging surprises. I picture many a reader coming across something on these pages that at first looks obscure or forbidding, but then, after a slightly longer look, makes sense and inspires an "aha!" There are many occasions for "aha-ing!" in these books. One can also wager that many a reader will come away from the encounters thinking, "I never knew that!" or "I never thought of that before." And they will be more ready than they had been to meet strangers of other faiths in a world that so many faiths *have* to share, or that they *get* to share.

Martin E. Marty
The University of Chicago

Preface

Ann Marie B. Bahr

The majority of people, both in the United States and around the world, consider religion to be an important part of their lives. Beyond its significance in individual lives, religion also plays an important role in war and peace, politics, social policy, ethics, and cultural expression. Yet few people feel well-prepared to carry on a conversation about religion with friends, colleagues, or their congressional delegation. The amount of knowledge people have about their own faith varies, but very few can lay claim to a solid understanding of a religion other than their own. As the world is drawn closer together by modern communications, and the religions of the world jostle each other in religiously plural societies, the lack of our ability to dialogue about this aspect of our lives results in intercultural conflict rather than cooperation. It means that individuals of different religious persuasions will either fight about their faiths or avoid the topic of religion altogether. Neither of these responses aids in the building of healthy, religiously plural societies. This gap in our knowledge is therefore significant, and grows increasingly more significant as religion plays a larger role in national and international politics.

The authors and editors of this series are dedicated to the task of helping to prepare present and future decision-makers to deal with religious pluralism in a healthy way. The objective scholarship found in these volumes will blunt the persuasive power of popular misinformation. The time is short, however. Even now, nations are dividing along religious lines, and "neutral" states as well as partisan religious organizations are precariously, if not always intentionally, tipping delicate balances of power in favor of one religious group or another with doles of aid and support for certain policies or political leaders. Intervention in the affairs of other nations is always a risky business, but doing it without understanding of the religious sensitivities of the populace dramatically increases the chances that even well-intentioned intervention will be perceived as political coercion or cultural invasion. With such signs of ignorance already manifest, the day of reckoning for educational policies that ignore the study of the world's religions cannot be far off.

This series is designed to bring religious studies scholarship to the leaders of today and tomorrow. It aims to answer the questions that students, educators, policymakers, parents, and citizens might have about the new religious milieu in which we find ourselves. For example, a person hearing about a religion that is foreign to him or her might want answers to questions like these:

- How many people believe in this religion? What is its geographic distribution? When, where, and how did it originate?

- What are its beliefs and teachings? How do believers worship or otherwise practice their faith?

- What are the primary means of social reinforcement? How do believers educate their youth? What are their most important communal celebrations?

- What are the cultural expressions of this religion? Has it inspired certain styles of art, architecture, literature, or music? Conversely, does it avoid art, literature, or music for religious reasons? Is it associated with elements of popular culture?

- How do the people who belong to this religion remember the past? What have been the most significant moments in their history?

- What are the most salient features of this religion today? What is likely to be its future?

We have attempted to provide as broad coverage as possible of the various religious forces currently shaping the planet. Judaism, Christianity, Islam, Hinduism, Buddhism, Confucianism, Taoism, Sikhism, and Shinto have each been allocated an entire volume. In recognition of the fact that many smaller ancient and new traditions also exercise global influence, we present coverage of some of these in two additional volumes titled "Indigenous Religions" and "New Religions." Each volume in the series discusses demographics and geography, founder or foundational period, scriptures, worldview, worship or practice, growing up in the religion, cultural expressions, calendar and holidays, history, and the religion in the world today.

The books in this series are written by scholars. Their approach to their subject matter is neutral and objective. They are not trying to convert readers to the religion they are describing. Most scholars, however, value the religion they have chosen to study, so you can expect the general tone of these books to be appreciative rather than critical.

Religious studies scholars are experts in their field, but they are not critics in the same sense in which one might be an art, film, or literary critic. Religious studies scholars feel obligated to describe a tradition faithfully and accurately, and to interpret it in a way that will allow nonbelievers as well as believers to grasp its essential structure, but they do not feel compelled to pass judgment on it. Their goal is to increase knowledge and understanding.

Academic writing has a reputation for being dry and uninspiring. If so, religious studies scholarship is an exception. Scholars of religion have the happy task of describing the words and deeds of some of the world's most amazing people: founders, prophets, sages, saints, martyrs, and bodhisattvas.

The power of religion moves us. Today, as in centuries past, people thrill to the ethical vision of Confucianism, or the dancing beauty of Hinduism's images of the divine. They are challenged by the one, holy God of the Jews, and comforted by the saving promise of Christianity. They are inspired by the stark purity of

Islam, by the resilience of tribal religions, by the energy and innovation of the new religions. The religions have retained such a strong hold on so many people's lives over such a long period of time largely because they are unforgettable.

Religious ideas, institutions, and professions are among the oldest in humanity's history. They have outlasted the world's great empires. Their authority and influence have endured far beyond that of Earth's greatest philosophers, military leaders, social engineers, or politicians. It is this that makes them so attractive to those who seek power and influence, whether such people intend to use their power and influence for good or evil. Unfortunately, in the hands of the wrong person, religious ideas might as easily be responsible for the destruction of the world as for its salvation. All that stands between us and that outcome is the knowledge of the general populace. In this as in any other field, people must be able to critically assess what they are being told.

The authors and editors of this series hope that all who seek to wield the tremendous powers of religion will do so with unselfish and noble intent. Knowing how unlikely it is that that will always be the case, we seek to provide the basic knowledge necessary to critically assess the degree to which contemporary religious claims are congruent with the history, scriptures, and genius of the traditions they are supposed to represent.

Ann Marie B. Bahr
South Dakota State University

1

Why Study New Religious Movements?

These fruitless strifes, these ruinous wars shall pass away,
and the "Most Great Peace" shall come.

—The Promise of World Peace,
Universal House of Justice, Baha'i

M any people wonder why anyone would bother learning about New Religious Movements. It is a good question to which there are several good answers. First, New Religious Movements are interesting because they often provide creative and alternative ways of answering questions of "ultimate concern." Secondly, New Religious Movements often represent areas of cultural conflict and questioning. Third, New Religious Movements can provide insight into the development of established religions. Finally, studying New Religious Movements can provide ways to see where and how societies are changing or resisting change.

NEW RELIGIOUS MOVEMENTS ARE INTERESTING
New Religious Movements often develop creative and unique ways of understanding and answering the "big" questions of life: Who am I? What am I doing here? Where am I going? Why do certain things (bad or good) seem to happen? What is my place in the world supposed to be? Is there really any larger meaning or purpose to life, and if there is, how am I supposed to figure it out? Does anything exist beyond death? These questions are what theologian Paul Tillich called issues of ultimate concern for most people. Many times the leaders and adherents of New Religious Movements are willing to "try on" and meaningfully confront questions of ultimate concern with which mainstream religious bodies are not entirely comfortable, such as issues of gender, sexuality, and politics. New Religious Movements are often willing to experiment and develop different answers to these questions of ultimate concern. As a result, New Religious Movements can provide meaning and purpose to individuals who, for reasons of political and economic displacement, trauma, education, or other kinds of social exclusion, may have come to experience profound dissatisfaction with traditional religious options offered in their communities.

NEW RELIGIOUS MOVEMENTS ADDRESS CULTURAL CONFLICT AND QUESTIONING
New Religious Movements often arise out of a deep sense of

cultural, personal, and social unease. Sometimes social and political upheaval stemming from war, severe economic turmoil, or a series of natural disasters triggers the emergence of New Religious Movements. In fact, many scholars point to the turbulent times of the late Roman Empire as an example of the kind of political and social turmoil that made Christianity, both as a personal religion and a principle of social organization, so attractive. At the same time, it seems that the development of New Religious Movements also requires a level of relative cultural openness, technological sophistication, and even affluence. Cultural openness leads to the introduction of new ideas that some people will embrace and others will oppose, finding them foreign and frightening. Studying New Religious Movements can provide insight about where a culture is conflicted within itself and where a society may or may not be addressing internal or external issues of control or difference.

SECTS, CULTS, TRADITION, AND RELIGION

Before discussing the third reason for studying New Religious Movements, it is important to become familiar with two common terms: *sect* and *cult*. You may hear someone say that the Church of Latter-day Saints (Mormons) is a "sect" of Christianity and that Scientology or Hare Krishna are examples of "cults." Terms used in this way, without any further information, do not really tell us anything about the religious movements themselves. Instead, they merely give some indication of what the speaker might believe or think about these movements. "Cult," in particular, is often used in a very negative way in the media and tends to conjure up pictures of brainwashed disciples blindly following fanatical leaders who steal souls and money in an attempt to gather as much personal power as possible—even up to the point of leading their followers to their deaths. "Sect" has a less pejorative implication but is still often used to describe a movement that is considered deviant from a presumed norm, even if such a movement—for example, the Church of Latter-day Saints—has become a respectable church that contributes much to American society. In Europe, the term sect often has the same meaning as cult in the United States. For these reasons, neither term will be used to describe the New Religious Movements discussed in this book. Instead, the terms *emergent, new, alternative, faith group, faith community, movement,* or *religion* will be used in a flexible manner.

Even determining when a religion is "new" is often a matter of context and definition. When, for example, does an "emergent religious movement" simply become a "religion"? This is an important question for scholars. A new religion is always a religion; it is just "new" in relationship to a larger society out of which it emerges or, in some cases, encounters, as when an established religion like Buddhism comes to the United States. A New Religious Movement may cease to be "new" when it becomes the dominant religion of a culture, or it becomes such a regular feature of that culture that it is no longer novel. Certain civilizations have a long history of constantly evolving New Religious Movements. Indian society, for example, has come to expect new gurus, teachers, and schools. In India, a religious movement or guru really has to stand out in some way to be recognized as new or different. It is also important when thinking about these terms to consider that many of the great world religions, such as Christianity, Islam, and Buddhism, started out as New Religious Movements. In fact, it can be argued that Christianity and Islam began as "cults" based on the teachings of a particular individual or prophet and that these cults, for a variety of historical and political reasons, eventually emerged as dominant world religions. Buddhism is often understood as a religious and philosophical sect that split from the main body of Hindu teaching rather than a cult, even though the movement was started by the insights of one man. Many Hindus regard Buddhism in precisely this way, as a distinct and particular way of practicing Hinduism according to the teachings and experiences of one person.

Another useful term is *tradition.* In common American English, religion is generally understood to be an entire church or tradition. We can talk about the Roman Catholic Church as a distinct body. We can also talk about Christian tradition as an entire set of churches that are all centered around the image or teachings of Jesus of Nazareth, understood as "Christ," of which the Roman Catholic Church is a part. For certain Protestants, the Roman Catholic Church may not be considered part of their Christian tradition, so they will talk about the "Roman Catholic religion" as being separate from their own. For most scholars of religion, however, Protestants and Catholics, as well as any number of other groups, may be considered to be part of the Christian tradition. In other words, a group is considered to be part of a tradition (Buddhist, Christian, Islamic, etc.) based solely on how that particular group understands itself. Thus, for most scholars of religion, a statement that Latter-day Saints or Roman Catholics are not "of the Christian religion" would be considered inaccurate.

A "movement" is an even broader concept and usually refers to many small groups that are organized around a set of principles, a number of teachers, or a collection of texts. For example, you may have heard about the New Age Movement so many times that it seems like an established tradition, yet there is no one New Age church, or leader, or set of texts. If you were to ask ten New Agers what the New Age is, or what teachers they follow, you would probably get at least ten different answers. Out of this assortment of beliefs and followers, however, a number of distinct groups have emerged (in some cases, many have already disappeared). This is true of the Neo-Pagan/Wicca movement, which will be discussed later, but historical evidence suggests that Christianity may have emerged out of similar social and cultural circumstances. There were many Jewish religious groups with varying ideas of what "messiah" might mean, and there were even many claimants for the role of messiah. Christianity emerged as one of the success stories (there are actually other success stories from that period as well, Rabbinical Judaism and the Mandeans being the most notable). Thus, a movement, in and of itself, may or may not evolve into a distinct religious tradition or church.

STUDYING NEW RELIGIOUS MOVEMENTS CAN HELP EXPLAIN THE ORIGINS OF ESTABLISHED RELIGIONS

Developing this historical perspective of traditions and movements is in no way intended to diminish or impugn the achievements and influence of major religious bodies. Instead, such a perspective is essential for understanding the third and fourth reasons that it is important to study New Religious Movements. New Religious Movements can provide clues about the beginnings of more established religions. New Religious Movements serve as reminders that what appears inevitable, may not seem so obvious when available evidence is examined. It is easy for present-day Christians or Muslims to look at their respective histories and experience what for them is a sensation of historical destiny. However, when historians and archaeologists actually sift through the ruins and records of first- and second-century Roman society, the inevitability of Christian triumph is not so readily apparent in the data. Many Christians at the time were fairly confident that their movements would be successful, but many of them also admitted that earthly victory was not certain. This could explain why there was such an emphasis on the Kingdom of Heaven to come and the return of Christ among early Christians.

The available evidence indicates that early Christian communities and the early community founded by Muhammad encountered many, if not all of the same, trials and tribulations that New Religious Movements face today. These include social suspicion and persecution, the "crisis of succession" (what happens when the leader dies?), and lack of consensus about what the leader really said or meant. Many New Religious Movements even have major controversies about the nature of their scriptures or the correct organization of their institutions in much the same way that the fourth-century Christian Church did. Studying recent and current New Religious Movements can provide invaluable insights into the dynamics of how such difficulties were worked out in the major religions and can also help answer other questions: Why are some religious movements successful and others not? What does a successful religion or religious movement look like? What ultimate concerns must it address to be successful? How do successful religious movements address questions of ultimate concern?

NEW RELIGIOUS MOVEMENTS CAN INDICATE WHERE CULTURES ARE CHANGING OR RESISTING CHANGE

Finally, keeping all of the above in mind, we can move on to the fourth reason to study New Religious Movements. New Religious Movements provide a glimpse of those places where a culture is both changing and resisting change. One cannot assume that what is "new" today will not be "dominant" tomorrow. In fact, it is precisely this concern that has often led to the vilification and persecution of New Religious Movements, past and present. As previously noted, New Religious Movements seem to require at least two conditions that allow them to take root, develop, and be successful. There must be access to alternative sources of spiritual meaning (openness and relative tolerance), and there must also be, at least most of the time, a general condition of change, upheaval, or social mobility (dislocation). Although many modern cultures have embraced rapid change, the very nature of such change suggests that old ways of seeing the world, as embodied in traditional religious structures, no longer adequately answers questions of ultimate concern.

New Religious Movements tend to emerge where large numbers of people are dissatisfied with the way things are and find available, alternative ways of answering these questions of ultimate concern through texts, other cultures, or innovative individuals. These new ways of answering such questions of ultimate concern may not be in accord with established tradition, but they can succeed nonetheless, depending on how the real conditions of the lives of dissatisfied people are addressed by the New Religious Movements. Therefore, a study of New Religious Movements should involve a close look at the tension between the continuous need of many people to have their ultimate concerns answered (particularly in light of ever more rapidly changing societies impacted by technology, science, political, and economic change), and the relative willingness of traditional religious bodies to address those concerns directly.

ARE NEW RELIGIOUS MOVEMENTS DESTRUCTIVE OR VIOLENT?

It is true that there are a few New Religious Movements that end up in situations that most would consider destructive or violent. In fact, some New Religious Movements have been destructive in some way. These include the Branch Davidians in Waco, Texas; the Aum Shinri Kyo group in Japan, which staged a terrorist attack on a commuter train a few years back; or the Heaven's Gate members who killed themselves in a mass suicide gesture. The emphasis here, however, should be on the word "few." Most New Religious Movements are so short-lived that they do not have the time to become fanatical or destructive.

For example, in the first three decades of nineteenth-century America, there were scores of new Christian movements that sprang up as the frontier of the nation moved west. Many of these movements had names that only scholars know about today, for example, the Sixth-Principle Baptists, Ephrata, The Rogerians, and The Seekers. Most of these groups were eventually absorbed into larger emerging Christian denominations, such as the Methodists or the Disciples of Christ. A couple of these groups, The Millerites and the Latter-day Saints, developed into religious bodies of their own and became The Seventh-day Adventists and the Church of Jesus Christ of Latter-day Saints. Although there were many religious revivals among all of these groups, most instances of violence were committed by mainstream Christians against members of these groups and not by the groups themselves. The vast majority of followers of New Religious Movements are not interested in committing violence; they simply want their questions of ultimate concern addressed. When looking at issues of violence and New Religious Movements, it is important to keep a levelheaded perspective.

In 2003, it was estimated that there were about 2,700 different religious groups in the United States, most of them qualifying as New Religious Movements. Very few of these have made headlines because of violent or destructive behavior. Chances are, most people have not heard about more than one or two, and they are probably related to the examples listed above.

By the same token, religions, whether new or established, are living entities and not simply products of culture. It is possible for an established religion to decline and die. One of the best examples of this is the historically known world religion of Manichaeism that was founded by the Persian prophet Mani in the third century A.D. Manichaeism spread from Europe to China and was a major rival of Christianity in the late Roman Empire. Once Christianity became the official religion of the empire, most other religions were outlawed, and Manichaeism was especially persecuted. In the East, however, Manichaeism remained alive and influential in places like present-day Afghanistan. There are some reports that it survived in China until the sixteenth century. The death of a religion does not necessarily signal that it was wrong or self-destructive. It may simply have become irrelevant, or it was replaced by another faith, or, as in the case of Manichaeism in the West, it was outlawed and persecuted.

The New Religious Movements that have been chosen for this volume run the gamut from well-established, recently emerged churches or religions, such as the Church of Jesus Christ of Latter-day Saints and Baha'i Faith, to very loosely organized movements, such as Neo-Pagans or Wiccans. We will examine religions that have branched off from Christian and Buddhist sources, and others, such as Ifa, which started out as an indigenous religion and is now in the process of becoming a new world faith through internationalization, colonialism, and globalism. Although the bulk of scholars who study New Religious Movements focus on the United States, the fact is that New Religious Movements are springing up all over the globe. As more and more people become aware of the spiritual and religious possibilities open to them by travel, commerce, and the Internet, the rise and development of New Religious Movements is truly becoming a global and international event. It promises to become even more complex and varied as the world continues to change. Knowing about these emergent religions is an important component of knowing about the people who share this planet with you. This is particularly vital today because religion is increasingly becoming a source of conflict in many regions of the world.

2

The Church of Jesus Christ of Latter-Day Saints

And I have put my words in thy mouth,
and have covered thee in the shadow of mine hand,
that I may plant the heavens and lay the
foundations of the Herat, and say unto Zion:
Behold, thou art my people.

—Book of Mormon, 2 Nephi 8:16
Translated by Joseph Smith

INTRODUCTION

The Church of Jesus Christ of Latter-day Saints (LDS) constitutes the largest and most successful of American New Religious Movements. Since its inception in 1830, the Church has grown at a steady rate of approximately 2 percent per year. As of 2003, the official membership claim of the Church stood at about just under 12 million, with a slight majority outside the United States. There are 20,000 LDS churches and 116 temples in 150 countries. Sizable populations can be found in western Canada, South America, and parts of Europe. In 2003, *U.S. News and World Report* reported that, at present rates of growth, LDS membership—which is already among the top 10 in the United States—could reach 265 million by the end of the twenty-first century.

Although most commonly called "Mormons" by their neighbors and the media, Church members prefer to be known by their official name. In 2001, the leadership of the Church asked that the media refer to them by their full name. To honor this request, this chapter will use the term *Latter-day Saints*, *LDS*, or *Saints*, when referring to the Church and individual members. Use of the term *Mormon* has been retained in some circumstances for historical or grammatical reasons. The Reorganized Church of Latter-day Saints, a smaller Mormon-faith community that dates from the time of founder Joseph Smith's death, has asked the media to refer to them as the Community of Christ to distinguish themselves from the Church of Jesus Christ of Latter-day Saints. Their request is also honored in this chapter. Both churches refer to non-Saints as Gentiles, and this usage has also been retained in some instances.

FOUNDATIONS

In 1820, in the upstate New York town of Palmyra, a young man named Joseph Smith began to have a series of visions. At the same time, Smith was concerned over which church to join. As was the custom during that period of American history, Baptist, Presbyterian, and Methodist congregations were conducting a series of revivals in order to generate new membership. Smith's family had a long history of religious searching. Smith's father had raised his children with the idea of religious liberty and stressed the importance of freedom to search for God's truth wherever it might be found. Under the revivalist pressure of the local churches, however, various members of Smith's family began to convert to Presbyterianism. Smith toyed briefly with the idea of joining the Methodist Church but was not convinced. Finally, he decided to take the question to God. So he prayed. According to his own account of what occurred next, God the Father and Jesus appeared before him and explained that none of the churches represented the true church. He was not to become a member of any church but was to wait for a special assignment that would soon be given to him.

According to the official LDS account of the key event, in 1823, Smith was visited three times by the angel Moroni. This divine being showed Smith where he could find a set of golden tablets that contained a previously unknown history of the original peoples of the American continents. The plates were located under a large rock, on a hill that many scholars believe is an ancient Indian mound that Smith later referred to as Cumorah. At the site, Smith was also shown the "Urim and Thummim," a device that enabled him to read the mysterious script contained on the golden plates. He reportedly also found

SECOND GREAT AWAKENING

Scholars who study American Religion often refer to the time period between 1790 and 1845 as the "Second Great Awakening." This period, a time of great growth and turbulence in American society in general, saw an explosion of New Religious Movements. Some of the these new movements led to prominent American denominations, such as the Church of Jesus Christ of Latter-day Saints, the Disciples of Christ, and the Seventh-day Adventists. Many were responses to revivals conducted by Baptists, Methodists, and Presbyterians.

brass plates containing quotations from the Hebrew Scriptures, genealogies, and an Israelite breastplate. The divine being insisted that Smith could not take possession of the objects for another four years and that he was to visit the objects every year at the autumnal equinox.

In 1827, with the objects in hand, Smith began the process of translating the plates, which were written in what was later called "reformed Egyptian" (Experts say there is no known form of this reported language.) Smith's wife Emma and two of his associates, Martin Harris and Oliver Cowdery, served as assistants and scribes. They later signed an affidavit attesting to the existence of the plates. Subsequent reported visitations by John the Baptist and various apostles enabled Smith and Cowdery to learn about reestablishing the priest-hoods of Aaron and Melchizedek and how to baptize each other in the true church. In 1830, the translated plates became The Book of Mormon or the "golden bible," as it was often called in the local press, and was presented to the world. Within a year, the Church of Jesus Christ of Latter-day Saints had attracted one thousand members.

The early years of the Latter-day Saints were filled with wandering and persecution. They tried to settle in Kirtland, Ohio, and then in Jackson County, Missouri. It was in Jackson County that Joseph Smith is said to have made his famous prediction that Christ would return to the city now called Independence. He called the location Zion. Wherever the Saints went, they were harassed by their neighbors. The state of Missouri even sponsored militias to drive the Saints from their homes and take their property, and many of the Saints died of exposure during the winter months. Still, the Church continued to grow. The Saints tried to settle in the town of Far West, Missouri, but in 1838, many were killed in a state-condoned massacre. The Saints organized their own militias for protection but were then accused of committing violence of their own. After the state's governor issued an order to exterminate them, the Saints finally left Missouri for a town in Illinois, which Smith renamed Nauvoo. It was in Nauvoo that Smith declared his revelation advocating the practice of polygyny, the taking of multiple wives.

In 1844, Smith decided to run for president of the United States. He had appealed to President Martin Van Buren directly for protection, and the president had disdainfully rejected his appeal. Those opposed to Smith (including some former members of the Church) printed articles critical of his political beliefs and about his still officially secret advocacy of polygyny. Smith arranged for the printing presses of those involved to be destroyed and was arrested along with his brother Hyrum. A lynch mob broke into the jail where the two were being held and killed them both. The death of Joseph Smith created a crisis that would split the Church irrevocably.

One of the unique features of Smith's life as a prophet was that, from the beginning, he always shared the power and responsibility of prophecy with a close-knit group of associates. Prophecy was not simply to be given and received; it was necessary that it be declared and worked out in an elite group. By the time of his death, Smith had already established the fundamentals of Latter-day Saints Church structure, the principles of which are detailed in a collection of revelations called Doctrine & Covenants. Thus, although the congregation was in crisis, its leaders had a basic plan of action they could follow. This did not quell all disagreements, however. Smith's closest associates, the Twelve Apostles (a group that is now called the Quorum of Twelve), met and prayed for guidance.

POLYGAMY/POLYGYNY

Polygamy is the taking of multiple husbands or wives. Polygyny refers only to the taking of multiple wives. Although the practice of plural marriage among the Latter-day Saints actually involved only the taking of multiple wives, the practice is often incorrectly referred to as polygamy. Mormon women were not allowed to take multiple husbands—a practice called polyandry.

According to Latter-day-Saint history, God revealed that Brigham Young, one of Smith's closest allies, should be the next leader of the community. After some initial reluctance, Brigham Young accepted the responsibility and led most of the Saints (about 19,000) from Nauvoo on a long, torturous trek to an area near the Great Salt Lake in what would later become the state of Utah. The Saints were understandably suspicious of other Americans and the federal government in particular, and they set up their city in a desert that was outside the legal boundary of the United States. They intended to make their Church an alternative political and religious organization.

Some Saints opposed the selection of Brigham Young and split from the Church. The majority of these formed another religious organization now called the Community of Christ (formerly the Reorganized Church of Jesus Christ of Latter-day Saints). Smith's first wife, Emma, and Joseph Smith III, one of Smith's sons, originally led the new religious community. The Community of Christ retained control of title over the Kirtland Temple in Ohio, most of the temple lot in Independence, Missouri (where they relocated in 1920), and the rest of Joseph Smith's property, despite legal efforts by the Latter-day Saints in Utah to regain partial control of these assets. The Community of Christ Temple site was dedicated in Independence, Missouri, in 1994, and the group maintains Kirtland Temple as a historical monument. They are very active in mission work and now claim about 250,000 members in 40 countries, although they have grown more slowly than the Utah Church. The Community of Christ has become more liberal and ecumenical in recent years, while the Latter-day Saints have tended toward what they consider a socially acceptable conservatism. Furthermore, the Community of Christ has generally rejected the use of the term *Mormon* to describe their community. There are also at least one hundred other related faith communities, some with memberships of only a few hundred, which can trace their origins from Joseph Smith and The Book of Mormon.

SCRIPTURES

The Church of Jesus Christ of Latter-day Saints considers several texts to be canonical (accepted as Scripture). The Old and New Testaments, as found in the King James Bible, are considered to be divinely inspired scripture, as is The Book of Mormon, which is held to be the continuation of God's historic work as recorded in the Bible.

The Book of Mormon claims to reveal the true and previously hidden history of the Indians of North and South America, as well as the ministry of Jesus Christ in the Western Hemisphere. According to the book, one of the original peoples that scattered after attempting to construct the Tower of Babel settled in eastern Central America. They were called the Jaredites, and they were destroyed because of their wickedness. The ruins of their civilization can still be seen. The book further explains that about 600 B.C., immediately before the children of Israel were taken into exile in Babylon, some Israelites fled to the Americas. The Israelite patriarch Lehi and his two sons, Nephi and Laman, were among those who escaped. Separate tribes descended from Nephi and Laman, and these two related peoples fought constantly against each other. In fact, The Book of Mormon is largely a chronicle of their battles and the various prophetic leaders that God sent to try to reconcile the two sides.

As The Book of Mormon explains, Lamanites rejected God and degenerated into a primitive state of living, having mixed with the degraded remnants of the Jaredites. After his resurrection, Jesus Christ appeared to the Nephites and the Lamanites, taught them the gospel, encouraged them to persevere, and chose twelve disciples from among them. Eventually, the Nephites, lighter in skin color than the Lamanites and considered more moral, were exterminated. This, however, occurred after Mormon, a prophet of the Nephites, wrote the history of these peoples on gold plates and preserved them in a fortified hill. According to Latter-day Saint history, these are the plates that Smith was directed to find and that he translated into The Book of Mormon. The surviving Lamanites were considered to be the ancestors of Native Americans, and God gave them red skin in order to differentiate them from the Nephites, as a sign of their degenerate nature.

The Book of Mormon operates on several levels. It completes the history of the children of Israel, the Indians, and the Latter-day Saints. Furthermore, it reveals that Jesus showed himself to the inhabitants of the New World, and by implication, demonstrated that the new nation (America) would be the site where Christ would begin to restore his kingdom on Earth. It describes the calling of the prophet, Joseph Smith, who, in being chosen to find and translate the book, was entrusted with the task of reestablishing Christ's church on Earth. Lastly, some believe that The Book of Mormon actually corrects the Bible in some respects, because it completes and clarifies the Old and New Testaments.

Many Latter-day Saints believe that unscrupulous people have corrupted the text of the Bible during its long history and that distortions of grammar and meaning have crept in, making interpretation difficult. It is held that The Book of Mormon and an amended translation of portions of the Old and New Testaments by Joseph Smith correct the process of corruption and provide clues for true interpretation of biblical text.

In addition to The Book of Mormon, Latter-day Saints revere a text called Doctrine & Covenants, a series of prophetic utterances by Joseph Smith and others concerning questions of everyday morality and the organization of the Church. Because the Church believes in ongoing prophecy, revelations or "declarations" can be added to Doctrine & Covenants. The most recent prophetic declaration to be added was a 1978 decision that allowed African males to be admitted into the priesthood. The president of the Church, who is regarded as both a political leader and the ultimate apostle vested with prophetic power, normally "declares" such prophecies. His revelations are then confirmed by the Quorum of Twelve and become church doctrine.

The Church of Latter-day Saints and the Community of Christ each has its own apostolic traditions and its own presidents. For this reason, each church has its own version of

Doctrine & Covenants. Original revelations by Joseph Smith are retained in each version. The Community of Christ maintains that it has preserved more of Smith's original revelations. In March 2004, the president of the Community of Christ, W. Grant McMurray, was moved to issue a revelation concerning the prophetic mission of the Church. Although the language in the revelation is not precise, leaving it open for interpretation, the prophecy issued the challenge that the church "create new forms of ministry." McMurray's revelation continued, "Even as the One you follow reached out to those who were rejected and marginalized, so must the community that bears his name." This revelation was confirmed by the Community of Christ Quorum and now constitutes Section 162 of Doctrine &

LOST TRIBES OF ISRAEL AND QUESTIONS OF RACE

The idea that Native Americans originally descended from a Lost Tribe of Israelites was popular in the United States during Joseph Smith's lifetime. Indians do not appear in the Bible. This troubled Christians coming to the New World, and they tried to explain the existence of the Indians with this theory. Another popular racist theory held that people with dark skin, Africans and Indians, for example, exhibited the mark of Cain, a sign identifying their ancestors with the murder of the biblical figure of Abel. Both of these ideas appear in The Book of Mormon. Two excerpts from the Book of Mormon illustrate them:

And he [Lord God] had caused the cursing to come upon them, yea, even a sore cursing, because of their iniquity. For behold, they had hardened their hearts against him, that they had become like unto a flint; wherefore, as they were white, and exceedingly fair and delightsome, that they might not be enticing unto my people the Lord God did cause a skin of blackness to come upon them. (2 Nephi 5:21).

And their curse was taken from them, and their skin became white like unto the Nephites. (3 Nephi 2:15).

Covenants. In both communities, such declarations must be confirmed by the entire community at a biannual convention before it becomes binding.

The Church of Latter-day Saints also regards as scripture a collection called The Pearl of Great Price. The Pearl contains selections from The Book of Moses, The Book of Abraham, Writings of Joseph Smith, and a text called the The Articles of Faith, a document that Smith composed when he was asked by a journalist to summarize the beliefs of Latter-day Saints. The Community of Christ regards these texts as distorting Smith's revelations, in some cases introduced by the LDS church to justify the practice of polygamy, which has always been rejected by the church now known as the Community of Christ. The Latter-day Saints also value various historical works, some by Joseph Smith, but do not consider them scripture. Splinter Mormon-faith groups, such as the Church of Christ (Temple Lot), the Fundamentalist LDS Church (FLDS Church), and the Church of Jesus Christ (Bickertonite), accept the King James Bible and The Book of Mormon as scripture but vary widely regarding the other texts. It is worth noting that The Book of Mormon is accepted as revelation or at least historically significant by certain groups that are not affiliated with Mormon-faith communities. The Book of Mormon has been considered potential scripture by numerous UFO groups since the 1950s and has recently been discussed as revelation in various New Age communities.

WORLDVIEW

The Latter-day Saints and all other Mormon-faith groups share two main beliefs. The first is that the original church founded by Jesus Christ died out in the second century and was replaced by religious authorities who created the Roman Catholic, Eastern Orthodox, and later Protestant churches. The second shared belief is that this original church was "restored" by Joseph Smith in nineteenth-century America and is embodied in the structure and doctrine of the Latter-day Saints or the other Mormon-faith groups. This means that the Latter-day Saints are restorationists; they believe that their church alone represents the original teachings and intent of Jesus Christ. Restorationism is not unique to the Latter-day Saints. Many new Christian movements in the early nineteenth century maintained this view. In fact, many Puritan groups who came to the American colonies from England maintained the view that they—not the Anglican Church or Catholics—represented the restoring of Christ's true kingdom on Earth. Restorationism is also a common theme in Pentecostal and other fundamentalist Christian bodies even today. The main idea is that Christ's original message was distorted by human desires for power and needs to be restored.

The Latter-day Saints represent a unique position between premillennialist and postmillennialist conceptions of Christ's kingdom. They maintain the postmillennialist position that the Church of Latter-day Saints is the restored and true representation of Christ on Earth and argue the need to spread the gospel. Unlike most postmillennialist churches, however, the Saints also insist that the rule of Christ is an actual physical reign, usually a premillennialist view. As a result, the Saints are not as worried about when the physical return of Christ might occur. His church is already present, in an actual physical way, so there is no need for immediate concern. Although some Saints do maintain a belief about Christ's return being presaged by dramatic and possibly traumatic physical signs (earthquakes, climactic shift, or famine), most Saints do not emphasize this.

The most distinctive beliefs of the Saints concern the nature of deity, the composition of the afterlife, and the eternal nature of true marriage. The theology of the Latter-day Saints is considered nominally Trinitarian: God and Christ are separate physical deities who can appear individually, as they are said to have appeared to Joseph Smith. The Holy Spirit/Ghost is not physical and serves as a kind of prompter of conscience— encouraging people to behave morally. These three are considered "one in purpose and perfection" but quite separate otherwise. Smith declared that Jesus would return in Independence, Missouri, which is why the Community of Christ maintains its headquarters there.

Saints generally tend to believe in a form of universal salvation. Hell exists but is considered a place where individuals who have insisted on rejecting Christ after having a sure knowledge of his divinity are gradually trained and allowed to move into the lower regions of Heaven. Such people are referred to as the "sons of perdition."

Heaven consists of three levels: the Telestial Kingdom, where the wicked reside; the Terrestrial Kingdom, where the moral non-Saints reside; and the Celestial Kingdom, where moral, upstanding Saints reside. Jesus visits the Telestial Kingdom and assists the wicked in bettering themselves within that realm, but they cannot move up to other realms. The Celestial Kingdom has several levels, with the highest reserved for those Saints whose marriages are "sealed" in a Temple ceremony, insuring that they are married for all eternity. Such individuals eventually become gods and goddesses in their own right and are provided with worlds they can help create and govern (The Community of Christ rejects this particular teaching). The

PREMILLENNIALISM AND POSTMILLENNIALISM

Postmillennialist Christian churches maintain that they represent the true Church of Christ on Earth. They also maintain that Christ will not return until the gospel has been preached across the world and that Heaven and Earth must pass away, because Christ's true Kingdom is spiritual and not earthly. Most mainstream churches (Catholic, Lutheran, Methodist, etc.) are postmillennialist in orientation.

Premillennialist Christian churches maintain that Christ's Church has not yet come and that there are periods or cycles of salvation and/or tribulation on the earth. Christ's Church is generally recognized as being an actual physical reign. Christians who believe in the rapture and tribulation are premillennialist in orientation. Tim LaHaye's best-selling Left Behind series represents a popularization of premillennialist thought.

Church teaches that Satan is an actual being, and a recent survey of young Saints found that approximately 60 percent of them maintain this belief.

Although the Church allows for civil divorce and annulment of marriage, it very strongly recommends that all unions between Saints be sealed in a Temple ceremony. The Church teaches that all souls have always existed and go through a period of learning before becoming physical beings on Earth. God's intent is that each soul be married with another in an eternal bond. This insures that marriages and the families produced by such marriages are themselves eternal. In a sense, this is how the Saints envision the ongoing process of creation: Souls are eternally bound together in marriage and the family. When people die, they are reunited in the Celestial Kingdom and work together to create and govern new worlds, assisting God in the process of creation.

This view of Saints as being cocreators with God has several other implications. Most Saints can accept some idea of evolution, without accepting Darwinian evolution; whereas God is at the heart of the world, the idea that certain species in the world might change or evolve is not necessarily a problem. Saints also believe that although sin exists in the world by virtue of Adam's fall, each soul is responsible for its own salvation and is not tainted by original sin. After all, all souls existed before Adam's sin. Since souls always exist, before and after death, the Church teaches that it is possible to baptize people post-mortem (after death) in order to insure that such individuals can make it to the Celestial Kingdom. To this end, the Church has amassed the largest collection of genealogical information in the world in order to add to the ranks of those posthumously baptized. This has led to great controversy. When the Church began posthumously baptizing famous Jews and Holocaust victims, the American-Jewish community protested and demanded that this activity be stopped immediately and that Jewish names be removed from the baptismal roster. In 1995, the Latter-day Saints made a formal agreement to stop such baptisms by proxy and to remove Jewish names; the Church still allows present members to baptize any Jewish ancestors they may have. The Community of Christ does not recognize or allow baptism by proxy.

WORSHIP

In order to understand how worship functions in the Church of Latter-day Saints, it is important to get a basic understanding of Church structure. The Church has developed a very complex hierarchy containing multiple levels of authority. The core of the Church, its base unit, is considered to be the family, with the father as the head and mother as the prime caregiver. Both parents are considered responsible for raising the children. A group of families constitutes a "ward," (church) presided over by a male bishop (Latter-day Saints women cannot be ordained). The ward also contains the Aaronic priesthood, teenage boys of the community who have been empowered to prepare and administer the Lord's Supper, and the Melchizedek priesthood, an older and more exclusive group chosen from the Aaronic priesthood, whose members preside in leadership roles. Women's relief organizations are responsible for much youth education and assist ward families in need, and each ward has youth groups.

Several wards constitute a "stake," each with its own president. Several stakes are organized into "areas" and are presided over by Area Authorities. Although every ward is a church, only areas maintain the size to warrant the building of a temple. Overseeing all Area Authorities are the First and Second Quorum of Seventies, often called the General Authorities. The General Authorities oversee mission and church projects and the building of temples. Finally, there is the Quorum of Twelve, also called the Apostles, and the First President (Prophet), who is assisted by two counselors. Although women are excluded from this hierarchy, their relief societies follow a parallel structure from the ward to general level. The unique function of this structure allows for all Saints who want to be involved in the church to find some level of participation. Although final authority is vested in the First President, his leadership is tempered by his counselors and the apostles immediately below him. This allows for a sharing of prophetic authority that can be traced back to Joseph Smith.

Temple rituals are not public events. Ward meetings, however, are completely open. Members must follow the basic commandments of honesty and chastity in order to participate, and fully tithe 10 percent of one's gross income to the church. Latter-day Saints and Community of Christ congregations practice a form of baptism by immersion and a form of confirmation by the laying on of hands. One service at the Community of Christ Temple in Independence, Missouri, appeared to consist primarily of singing, recitation of church business, preparation for the sacrament of the Lord's Supper, and a short sermon by the bishop. It was explained that the service was in two parts; visitors could attend the first, which included a performance by the Temple Choir, but were asked to leave before the second service began.

Membership and ordination services are apparently more complex and visitors are often not allowed in Community of Christ Temple rituals. Some suggest that elements of these rituals may be derived from Freemasonry, thus accounting for the privacy. The Community of Christ recognizes eight sacraments: the Blessing of Children, Baptism, Communion, Administration to the Sick, Ordination to Priesthood, Marriage, Evangelists Blessing (for people going out on mission work), and Confirmation of Membership (most frequently administered to converts). In both the Latter-day Saints and Community of Christ communities, there are very specific private rituals for ordaining individuals into the quorum and the presidency.

At the private level, family and individual prayer and mediation are strongly encouraged as the basis of a moral and spiritual life. Devout Saints fast at least once a month as a form of spiritual discipline. The General Authorities encourage families to hold "family home evenings," informal family gatherings where group prayer, fellowship, gospel lessons, meals, and play can be conducted by family members together.

GROWING UP

The family is the absolute center in the organization of the Latter-day Saints. Families have the potential for eternal existence together in the Celestial Kingdom. Although not all Saints have huge families, children are a special focus of the church, and reproduction is encouraged. This is part of the reason for the continuing growth of the Church. Church literature and teaching encourages children to be obedient and moral and to marry within the faith; it prohibits the use of tobacco, alcohol, drugs, and other stimulants (such as coffee or tea). All children are encouraged to participate in youth relief groups and to prepare themselves to become full partners within the larger church structure—boys for eventual membership in the Aaronic priesthood and girls as educators or members of women's relief (charity) organizations. Education for girls and boys is strongly encouraged, and the Saints have founded numerous institutions of higher learning with Brigham Young University being the most notable.

The Church emphasizes thrift, charity, and personal and family self-sufficiency. Recent letters from current Latter-day Saints President Gordon B. Hinckley to the worldwide Church have stressed the need for members to learn how to garden and store food, to pay off all debts, and to become physically fit. (Hinckley believes that rough economic and political times are ahead.) The Church strongly discourages the practice of spanking, believing that violence begets violence and that disobedient children need to be encouraged and loved to perfection, not physically punished when they make a mistake. Young adults are expected to devote two years of their life to missionary work, a task that could take them anywhere in the world. Their families are expected to pay for the majority of expenses (though many Mormon children save money throughout their childhood), and it is actually considered a great honor in many

Mormon families to be supporting two or more children in missionary efforts, even if the economic strain is great. As previously mentioned, each family of Saints is expected to tithe 10 percent of family earnings to the Church. Additionally, when families fast, they are encouraged "to donate at least the cost of the skipped meals." The Church uses these funds to provide financial support to any Mormon family in need; it is a kind of reciprocal welfare system, organized through the bishop and women's and youth relief groups. No Mormon family ever has to worry about being "left out in the cold." Most Saints rarely date outside their faith and their divorce rate is the lowest of any Christian group in the United States.

CULTURAL EXPRESSIONS
From the earliest days in Mormon history, there has been a strong community interest in music and singing. At first, alternative lyrics reflecting the views of the Church were written to familiar tunes, but eventually the Latter-day Saints developed their own distinctive forms of hymnody. At the same time, the Saints have a long tradition respecting the cultural and artistic achievements of others and have little difficulty incorporating music, philosophy, or artwork from various cultural sources that they believe can enhance life and the appreciation of beauty. The best and most public example of this approach is seen in the organization of the Mormon Tabernacle Choir, easily one of the most impressive musical ensembles ever assembled. The great tabernacle complex in Salt Lake City, Utah, was built with precision to allow the choir and any speaker to perform on stage without amplification. The 360-member choir, composed entirely of volunteers, performs classical, popular, and Mormon choral music with or without a full orchestra. Their achievements have been impressive. In April 2004, the weekly broadcast of the Mormon Tabernacle Choir, *Music and the Spoken Word*, was given a special award by the National Association of Broadcasters for having successfully conducted the longest continuous broadcast show (the program has been

on the air since 1929) in American history. In November 2003, President George W. Bush awarded the Mormon Tabernacle Choir the highest accolade of artistic achievement granted by the U.S. government, The National Medal of Arts. Several of their recordings have achieved gold and platinum status.

Another arena in which many Latter-day Saints have distinguished themselves is in popular literature. A very popular fantasy/science fiction writer, Orson Scott Card (coauthor of the Ender series), is a dedicated Saint who often incorporates Mormon themes into his interpretations of fantasy American history. He has been quoted as saying that science fiction/fantasy writing is a perfect avenue of expression for Latter-day Saints because there is no other popular genre that allows for a person to talk about other worlds, extraterrestrial and spiritual, while also discussing issues of personal morality and ethics. Since Saints have no trouble believing in the existence of other worlds or inhabited planets, they would have little trouble with the concept of imagining and writing about them. Two other popular Latter-day Saint science fiction and fantasy writers are M. Shayne Bell and Dave Wolverton. According to a recent article in the *Salt Lake City Tribune* (August 24, 2003), current Mormon interest in science and speculative fiction can be traced to a notable professor, Marion "Doc" Smith (retired), who taught a science fiction literature class at Brigham Young University and encouraged his students to write. One of the largest science fiction conventions in the United States is held in Utah every year.

CALENDAR AND HOLIDAYS

Latter-day Saints observe Sabbath on Sunday, as do most other Christians. They also observe Christmas and Easter but not Advent or Lent. In the United States, they observe national holidays as well as any local or regional celebrations. The first Sunday of every month is considered a fast day, and every devout Saint will go to church meetings and refrain from eating for two consecutive meals. Instead of eating, they will donate money to the poor through one of their relief agencies. Latter-day Saints also observe certain holidays that are specific to them and that reflect elements of the life of Joseph Smith and the early history of the Church. Salt Lake City celebrates July 24 as Pioneer Day, commemorating the day Saints first arrived in Salt Lake Valley in 1847. April 6 is remembered as the date that Joseph Smith founded the Church of the Latter-day Saints in New York in 1830. Another date that merits commemoration is May 15, the day that John the Baptist is said to have visited Joseph Smith in 1829 to ordain him into and provide the authority for the Aaronic Priesthood. Anniversaries and personal birthdays are often times of high celebration in Mormon families because such commemorations highlight the importance of the family.

CONTROVERSIES

There remains a great deal of controversy surrounding the practice of polygyny in the early Mormon Church. Most Saints maintain that Joseph Smith advocated the practice out of economic necessity, that there were more women in his early Church than men, and that most Mormon men did not take more than one wife. Although the latter point is probably true, the true reasons for Smith advocating the practice are a little less clear. Anti-Church critics use this early practice of the Church in Utah to impugn the character of Joseph Smith and Brigham Young, but it may be best to simply accept Smith at his word—he maintained that his advocacy of the practice came to him through revelation. Furthermore, experimentation with sexual and marriage customs is not uncommon in New Religious Movements, and several Christian sects in the nineteenth century made attempts along these lines. The Shakers opted for absolute celibacy and division of society by gender. The Oneida Community founded by John Humphrey Noyes dabbled with a form of controlled spouse swapping.

It is not entirely clear what led Joseph Smith to understand God's revelation as a mandate for the practice of polygyny, but from the moment he did, it was controversial. In fact, this was the beginning of a series of community disagreements that would result in the various Mormon sectarian splits. After Smith's assassination in 1844, a group of followers, including Smith's first wife Emma (who had always opposed the revelation of polygyny) and one of his sons, organized what would become the Community of Christ. They maintain that the developed doctrine of polygyny, as practiced in the Utah church, was never what Smith had intended and represented a distortion of revelation by Brigham Young.

The practice of polygyny became one of the main reasons for opposition to the Latter-day Saints in the nineteenth century. The U.S. government initiated several attempts to try to quell the practice or even destroy the Church. The first of these involved sending federal troops to capture Salt Lake City in 1857. The Church, anticipating this attack, sent out troops of its own. In the tension of the moment, these troops massacred a wagon train of settlers heading for Oregon Territory; a truly tragic episode known to history as the Mountain Meadow Massacre. After the Civil War, as the United States was expanding into the West, the statehood of Utah was rejected several times because of the practice of polygyny. Federal authorities finally began a series of legal maneuvers to strip legal power from the Church. The Morrill Anti-Bigamy Law of 1862 and the Edmunds Act of 1882 stated that the federal government had the constitutional authority to define marriage, that first amendment rights did not extend to polygyny, and that the government had the right to revoke the citizenship of anyone practicing polygyny. The government revoked the citizenship of Mormons, dissolved the Church's institutional status, and began to seize its assets. In 1890, the fourth president of the Church, Wilford Woodruff, announced that a "Great Accommodation" would be made with the U.S. government and that the Church would suspend the practice of polygyny for an "indefinite period." Six years later, Utah was admitted to the Union as the forty-fifth state.

Official polygynous marriages continued to be sealed secretly in the Church until the 1920s. Today, although the Church officially condemns the practice and has excommunicated about ten thousand people for continuing polygyny, it tends not to assist federal authorities in locating individuals who reject the "Great Accommodation." It is estimated that about thirty thousand people in the western states of the United States continue to observe polygyny; the media often refers to these people as "fundamentalist Mormons." Most recently, the western Canadian states of British Columbia and Alberta have refrained from persecuting such groups. Although polygynous marriages are not legally recognized, many Canadians have expressed concerns about such prosecution violating constitutional protections of religious freedom and privacy.

IN THE WORLD TODAY

The Church of Jesus Christ of Latter-day Saints represents the single most visible and successful New Religious Movement in American history. Saints are increasingly becoming part of the American landscape and may well emerge as one of the most powerful religious communities in the next century. In the past twenty-five years, Latter-day Saints have sought to reach out more vigorously to other Christian denominations by stressing their political similarities to the conservative religious right: They oppose the Equal Rights Amendment, abortion, and equal rights for gay citizens. The Church has also tried to shed some of the racism implied in The Book of Mormon and traditional practice by admitting African Americans to full membership and by officially repudiating the old belief that nonwhite skin signifies the mark of Cain. The 2002 Winter Olympics in Salt Lake City presented an opportunity for the Church to really come into its own. The spectacular opening and closing cere-monies, which featured the story of the Latter-day Saints as a special group of godly pioneers, showcased the larger acceptance of Saints in the fabric of American life. This does not mean, however, that opposition to the Latter-day Saints has ceased.

In the last decade, the United Methodist Church, the Presbyterian Church (USA), and the Southern Baptist Convention have all issued official statements criticizing or even condemning Latter-day Saints. These critiques have taken many forms, including attacks on the Book of Mormon, the person of Joseph Smith, or on the theology, practices, or even motives of the Latter-day Saints. Some Christian commentators have gone as far as identifying the Church of Latter-day Saints as a "dangerous cult" with "deviant" practices that use "brainwashing" techniques. In the summer of 1998, the Southern Baptist Convention sponsored a "Cross Over Salt Lake City," and members went door-to-door trying to convert as many Mormons (and other non-Baptists) as they could. None of this deters Latter-day Saints from continuing their mission to embody the Church of Jesus Christ on Earth, restored. They have organized well and will continue to practice their religion.

3

The Baha'i Faith

Let each morn be better than its eve
and each morrow richer than its yesterday.
Man's merit lieth in service and virtue
and not in the pageantry of wealth and riches.

—Baha'u'llah, "Tablet of Wisdom"

INTRODUCTION

According to their most recent estimates, the Baha'is number approximately 5 million members (84,000 adults in the United States) and have communities in 235 countries, making them one of the most widespread New Religious Movements in distribution if not in numbers. Their singular achievement has been to succeed in maintaining a new religion that emerged in the Middle East, amid controversy and continuing social conflict, and to spread this faith to a wide and diverse range of people. Indeed, the Baha'is may constitute one of the most ethnically diverse of the New Religious Movements, and this reflects one of the goals and values of the greater Baha'i community: to create a religion of unity and harmony among all the peoples on Earth. For the Baha'is, this goal of unity and harmony is part of the rich and diverse religious legacy of the religion's birthplace, Iran (Persia).

FOUNDATIONS

In the mid-nineteenth century, Iran was an impoverished country with a rich cultural and religious heritage. Most people in the West are still unaware of the great importance of old Persia as a place where Jews, Christians, and Muslims often coexisted peacefully, building rich cities out of the desert. Even before these commonly recognized religions existed, Persia was the location of one of the most influential yet little-known religious traditions in human history, Zoroastrianism. The impact of the Zoroastrian King Cyrus on world civilization cannot be overstated. The Hebrew Bible (Old Testament) actually uses the term *moshiach* (messiah) to describe Cyrus; such was his importance to ancient Jewish peoples. Other historically significant religions, such as Manichaeism, also originated in Persia (Iran).

In the middle of the nineteenth century, however, Iran was poor, neglected by both East and West, and torn apart by bitter tribal disputes between rival Shi'ah and Sunni Muslim factions. Both groups often took out their frustrations on Jewish, Christian, and Zoroastrian minorities. According to Baha'i history, in emulation and fulfillment of Persia's great prophetic past, a man whom history calls The Bab (meaning "door" or "gate") came into this troubled environment and began to preach a message of reconciliation. The Bab, whose given name was Ali Muhammad, called for an end to religious feuding, challenging the role of corrupt rulers who condoned the violence. He also said that all religious prophecy had led to a single end and

PERSIAN RELIGION

The ancient Persians were often considered by their neighbors, the Indians (South Asians), Babylonians, Greeks, and Israelites, to be among the most religious and wisest of people. Ancient Persians followed a religion that scholars call Zoroastrianism, a reform faith founded by the prophet Zarathustra. Many religious scholars argue that Zoroastrianism is probably one of the most influential and yet unacknowledged religions of the ancient world. Zoroastrians seemed to have first developed the religious idea of linear time, including the notion of a redeemer who would return to participate in a final great war between good and evil; ideas that fundamentally influenced Judaism, Christianity, and Islam.

Persia was also known in the ancient world as the land of the magi, or wise ones; generally astrologers who read the stars. From *magi* we get the terms *magic* and *magician*. Persia became known as a land from which many new religions emerged, including the worship of a Persian deity named Mithra. Mithra became so popular among Roman troops in the third and fourth centuries that the Emperor Constantine had to make Mithra's birthday, December 25, the official date of Christ's birth when Christianity became the state religion of Rome.

In the third century, the Persian prophet Mani founded a world religion, Manichaeism, which spread from Britain to China and Malaysia. The great Christian theologian Augustine studied Manichaeism before he was converted to Christianity, and Manichaeism was a major rival of the early Christian Church in the fourth and fifth centuries. Persia was also a land that was known for its relative religious tolerance. It was a civilization that included Jews, Christians, and Muslims, and many other religious minorities who all flourished there until the modern period.

that the time of the final new prophet was fast approaching. The Bab is said to have performed many righteous deeds. He gathered a group of followers, and his movement was called the Babi movement. He preached his message from May 23, 1844 to July 9, 1850, despite persecution, imprisonment, torture, and being denounced as a heretic. In July 1850, he was publicly executed with one of his followers.

After The Bab's death, official attention was turned to one of his staunchest supporters, a young man named Husayn Ali, who was imprisoned in Tehran. According to Ali, during a particularly difficult time in prison, the Holy Spirit came to him and revealed that he was the prophet of whom The Bab had spoken. In 1863, he was given the new name Baha'u'llah and came to understand that he was the final prophet, the Promised One that all religions of the world had foreseen. The shah (or king) exiled him to Baghdad, thinking that his removal would weaken his standing with local Babi believers. Baha'u'llah was then sent from city to city in the Ottoman Empire: to Istanbul, Adrianople, and finally to Akkar, Syria (now part of Israel). He lived in exile for almost twenty-two years.

Before leaving for Istanbul, Baha'u'llah revealed himself to his fellow Babis, and most of them accepted him as The Bab's foretold prophet. While in Baghdad, Baha'u'llah wrote one of the scriptures for which he has become known: The Book of Assurance (Kitab-i-Iqan). In this text, Baha'u'llah presented interpretations of the holy books of all faiths. His interpretations were intended to demonstrate that he was indeed the Promised One. In Adrianople, he composed a series of tablets in which he challenged the rulers of the day to fulfill their responsibilities to the people they ruled. It was while he was at Akkar, in a prison that had a truly dismal reputation, that Baha'u'llah is said to have achieved his greatest spiritual momentum. That period produced two of his most famous works: The Seven Valleys and Hidden Words, a collection of his prayers, meditations, and visions for organizing humanity. Hidden Words also contained instructions for establishing the organization of the Baha'i faith, insuring succession and a continuance of the message. These writings were smuggled outside the prison walls that held Baha'u'llah. Gradually, his movement began to grow.

Baha'u'llah appointed his son, Abdu'l-Baha, as his interpreter and as the successor who would carry on his revelatory and organizational work. Baha'u'llah died, while still in prison, in 1892. Abdu'l-Baha was also imprisoned by Ottoman authorities but was eventually released in 1908, after the first Western Baha'is began to arrive on pilgrimage to the Middle East. Upon his release, he arranged for the remains of The Bab—which had been secretly kept in Iran and other locations—to be interred in a tomb in what is now Haifa, Israel. He also arranged for the succession of the movement to be established through his grandson, Shoghi Effendi. Abdu'l-Baha died in 1921, leaving behind his own body of revealed writings and commentaries on his father's work.

SCRIPTURES

The Baha'is have a great number of scriptural writings bequeathed to them through Baha'u'llah, Abdu'l-Baha, and Shoghi Effendi. Perhaps the most famous of Baha'u'llah's writings are The Hidden Words, The Seven Valleys, The Most Holy Book, The Book of Certitude, and an anthology entitled Gleanings from the Writings of Baha'u'llah. The Hidden Words, originally written in Arabic, contains poetic utterances in which God appears to be speaking both to and through Baha'u'llah. The Seven Valleys is a collection of mystical contemplations in which Baha'u'llah describes stages on the spiritual path as a journey through seven valleys. The style of both texts is very similar to a long tradition of Islamic, mystical, Sufi poetry that exists in both Farsi (Persian) and Arabic. One of his earliest works, The Book of Assurance outlines his "great announcement." In this book, Baha'u'llah discussed the purpose of the history of the prophets and how and why he was chosen by God to be the manifestation that unites and fulfills all previous scriptures.

Abdu'l-Baha added to the corpus of revelation begun by his father by specifically addressing issues such as the ultimate unity between religion and science, racial harmony, and the equality of men and women in the Baha'i movement. Later, his grandson, Shoghi Effendi, compiled and translated many of the writings of Abdu'l-Baha and Baha'u'llah and wrote many commentaries on them, demonstrating how the teachings of each could be applied to everyday situations. Effendi's commentaries provide the guidance needed by the Universal House of Justice when it deliberates policies for the worldwide Baha'i movement. Together, the writings of The Bab, Baha'u'llah, Abdu'l-Baha, and Shoghi Effendi are considered by devout Baha'is to be revealed scripture.

WORLDVIEW AND ORGANIZATION

There are two main bodies that enshrine and consolidate the international Baha'i movement: the Guardianship and the Universal House of Justice. The Guardianship was secured by Shoghi Effendi, who was empowered by Abdu'l-Baha to apply his teachings and those of Baha'u'llah to the development and spread of the Baha'i faith. Effendi consolidated the teachings of his predecessors, developed extensive commentaries on them, and translated them from Arabic and Farsi into English. He also established the Universal House of Justice as directed by the teachings of Baha'u'llah and Abdu'l-Baha. Effendi died in 1957 with no heir, and because none of his followers met Baha'u'llah's strict requirements for succession, there is currently no living Baha'i Guardian. Effendi is still referred to as The Guardian.

The Universal House of Justice is the principal legislative body of the Baha'i movement. It was officially opened in 1963 when representatives from all the Baha'i bodies in the world met in Haifa, Israel, to choose nine from among their number to represent the global interests of all Baha'is. These representatives are elected every five years and they have several different mandates. In addition to representing Baha'is in their region, they are responsible for resolving difficulties, for overseeing mission work and outreach, and for determining how the Baha'is will respond to issues of national and international significance. Baha'u'llah stipulated that the representatives in the House of Justice should heed and respond to issues of humanitarian and global concern. He also instructed that the rulings of the House of Justice were to have the same authority as his own written words. The Universal House of Justice maintains the integrity of the writings of Baha'u'llah, Abdu'l-Baha, and Shoghi Effendi and rules on issues that are not specifically addressed in those texts. It can also change or reverse its rulings. For the Baha'is, the Universal House of Justice represents a material embodiment of what is called Baha'u'llah's Covenant: his unique vision and commitment to an absolute unity of humanity in the midst of diversity. This absolute unity is expressed in the following principles outlined by the Baha'i National Spiritual Assembly of the United States. The Universal House of Justice is to assist in uniting the world under the following precepts:

- Establishment of universal peace upheld by a world federal system

- Elimination of prejudice of all kinds

- Recognition of the equality of men and women

- Adoption of a universal auxiliary language

- Acceptance of the essential harmony of science and religion

- Implementation of universal compulsory education

- Application of spiritual solutions to the world's problems

Baha'u'llah is said to have absolutely provided for an authoritative transmission of teachings and a transfer of political and religious authority, thereby anticipating potential difficulties with succession and dissension. In this way, he established a materialization of his ideal of unity. Baha'is are to embody this ideal of unity in their dealings with each other and with all other human beings. Baha'is also believe that there will eventually be one government unifying all people on Earth. The Universal House of Justice is seen as a prototype of how such a one-world system of government might work. When a country achieves a "critical mass" of membership it may organize its own National Spiritual Assembly to supervise the community. There are currently seven National Assemblies worldwide. In each local community, if there are more than nine adult believers, local spiritual assemblies are elected to oversee the activities of that membership.

This ideal of unity is connected to the Baha'i conception of the unity of God and his manifestations. Many commentators have noted the similarities between elements of Islam and the Baha'i faith, but Baha'is point out that although there are similar elements found in Judaism and Christianity and between Hinduism and Buddhism, these are considered distinct religions. Baha'u'llah was undoubtedly influenced by the Iranian Islam of his day, but he also considered himself to be part of a line of prophets who traced their lineage far back into antiquity, a line that included revered figures who Muslims do not recognize, such as Buddha and Zarathustra. For Baha'is, the absolute oneness of God has revealed itself many times in history through select manifestations. Baha'u'llah is considered to be the ultimate of these manifestations and, as such, constitutes The Promised One who many other religions allude to and prophesy about, including the Messiah (Jewish/Christian), the Mahdi (Shi'ah Islam), the final Savior (Zoroastrianism), and Maitreya (*Mahayana Buddhism*). Baha'u'llah's message to humanity is that we are all one, and in him, God's final manifestation, all religions become one as well. He saw religious fighting, racism, and the divisions between men and women as three of the most insidious evils facing humanity. Even today, the central concern of many Baha'is is how to overcome divides of gender, race, ethnicity, and religious fanaticism. The Baha'is see themselves as promoting unity while protecting the diversities within their communities.

The Baha'is contribute to their spiritual community through participation and tithing. The official translation of Baha'u'llah's Book of Laws, Kitab-i-Aqdas, was first released in 1993, to the Western Baha'i communities. His ruling requiring a 19 percent tithe to be paid by all Baha'is to the Baha'i World Center on all surplus income was considered binding worldwide. So far, all Baha'i communities have responded positively to this ruling, and there has been no substantial drop in contributions.

There are no clergy, specific sacraments, or rituals in the Baha'i religion. Individual Baha'is are expected to pray every day, observe the nine holy days, and fast during the nineteen days preceding Naw Ruz, the Baha'i New Year. Furthermore, they are encouraged to work to eradicate all forms of prejudice and to see their work as a form of worship. If able, they are expected to make a pilgrimage—at least once in their lifetime—to the shrine where The Bab is buried, near the site where Baha'u'llah was imprisoned in present-day Israel. Finally, Baha'is are forbidden to consume alcohol. All organizational needs are run by individuals who are elected by spiritual assemblies to serve in particular capacities. In theory, except in the House of Justice, men and women can hold any office equally if they are elected to serve.

HOLIDAYS AND CEREMONIES

The Baha'is have a unique calendar that is composed of nineteen months of nineteen days each. Every year, there are four extra days that are celebrated as Intercalary days, or days that adjust the calendar. Each leap year, there is one extra Intercalary day, making five days. This period, lasting from February 25 to March 1, is called Ayyam-i-Ha and is considered a time of gift giving, charity, hospitality, and preparation for the fast preceding Naw Ruz.

The two most important festivals occur in the spring. In the nineteen days (one Baha'i month) prior to the spring equinox, Baha'is fast during the day and prepare themselves to enter into a new life by considering how they can grow spiritually in the coming year. Children under the age of fifteen, elderly individuals who are in poor health, pregnant or nursing mothers, or those who may be traveling are considered exempt from the fast. This is a daytime fast, from sunrise to sunset. The Baha'is celebrate Naw Ruz on the day of the spring equinox. Naw Ruz acts as a preparation for the most important festival of Rivdan, which is celebrated for twelve days, lasting from approximately April 21 to May 2. Rivdan marks the period during which Baha'u'llah revealed his mission as the manifestation of the Promised One prior to leaving Baghdad to serve out his permanent exile. According to the account, Baha'u'llah had gained the friendship of the ruler of Baghdad. When the appointed time came for Baha'u'llah to leave for Istanbul, the ruler allowed him to spend time in a pleasure garden, where he spoke to his disciples and followers and revealed his message. The ninth day of Rivdan was designated as the holiest day of the period by Baha'u'llah, and Baha'is also set apart the first and twelfth days of Rivdan as special, marking the beginning and ending of the festival.

Baha'is also commemorate May 23 as the Declaration of The Bab, the man who announced the coming of the Promised One and his new religion. July 9 is remembered as the day when The Bab was martyred in Tehran. Additionally, the Baha'is remember the birth and death anniversaries of the most important figures in the religion: November 12 is celebrated as the Birth of Baha'u'llah and May 29 commemorates Baha'u'llah's Ascension. October 10 is remembered as the birthday of The Bab. November 28 is commemorated as the day of Abdu'l-Baha's Ascension.

Since 1950, the Baha'is have been inviting other religious leaders to join them in celebrating World Religion Day, commemorated on the third Sunday in January. The purpose of World Religion Day is to encourage members of diverse religious communities to come together to discuss their harmony of spiritual principles and to confer about ways in which conflicts between faith communities can be addressed and resolved. For the Baha'is, world religion is the motivating force for world unity, because "religion should be the cause of love and agreement" between peoples and not a cause for dissension and fighting. Many large cities in the United States and abroad now host World Religion Day commemorations of their own.

CULTURAL EXPRESSIONS

From the start, the Baha'is have been especially keen to eliminate the divisions between men and women, as well as individuals of diverse races, ethnic groups, and religions. Because the principal message of Baha'u'llah is the true and ultimate unity of humanity, such divisions are seen as particularly antithetical to the purposes of God. The Baha'is sought early to reach out to individuals of diverse racial, ethnic, and religious backgrounds. Thus, what the Baha'is may lack in sheer numbers, they make up for in diversity. Indeed, African Americans were among the first Americans to be converted to the Baha'i faith in 1893. By the 1970s, approximately 30 percent of American Baha'is were African American. Native Americans have also been drawn to Baha'i, and there are several thousand Eskimo and Indian Baha'i who live in Alaska and on Navajo and Sioux reservations. Southeast Asian immigrants to the United States have also been drawn to the Baha'i movement. The Baha'is in the United States have a distinguished history of battling racism, and have been involved with the NAACP and the Urban League, two important civil rights organizations, for many years. In 1992, a representative of the National Spiritual Assembly was appointed to the rank of commissioner on the committee that oversaw the establishment of the Martin Luther King Federal Holiday. The bulk of American Baha'i membership, however, is drawn from the white Protestant middle class.

The Baha'i, as a group, are very interested in promoting the arts as a tool that can facilitate communication and interest among diverse groups. The Baha'i Association for the Arts (BAFA) is a large international group that fosters transnational communication between Baha'is of different nationalities. One example of how this works can be seen in the rapid acceptance of musical styles adopted by Baha'i communities across the world. In 1992, gospel singing was formally introduced to the Baha'i World Congress. The impact of gospel singers singing the praises of Baha'u'llah was so immediate that within three years, the lyrics of the songs were translated into multiple languages, which facilitated the songs being used by Baha'i groups for educational and devotional purposes from Russia to Malaysia.

FAMILIES AND CHILDREN

Children are considered to be adults in the Baha'i religion when they reach their fifteenth birthday. The responsibilities of being an adult Baha'i fall equally on male and female children alike. There is a brief ceremony that commemorates this rite of passage, but many Baha'i children simply mark the occasion the first time they participate in the fast prior to Naw Ruz. The Baha'is have developed many teaching programs focusing on children so that the young may be taught about Baha'u'llah and his successors. There are Websites that specifically focus on Baha'i materials for children.

There are also several national Baha'i schools with year-round programs for both adults and children. These include the Bosch Baha'i School in Santa Cruz, California, the Louhelen Baha'i School in Detroit, Michigan, the Green Acre Baha'i School in Maine, and the Louis G. Gregory Baha'i School in South Carolina. A special Native American Baha'i Institute is located on the Navajo Reservation in Arizona, and the Wilmette Institute, site of the U.S. National Spiritual Assembly, offers accredited college-level classes. Further information about child and young-adult programs can be found at the National Baha'i Education Website.

Each year, the curriculum is organized around a specific theme set by the Universal House of Justice. The theme for 2004–2005 was "Lighting the Way: Blazoning the Name of Baha'u'llah." The journal *Brilliant Star* is a special educational magazine that is geared toward the parents of children six to twelve years of age. It is published six times a year and is intended to encourage Baha'i children to strengthen their religious identity through history, ethics, and the principles of unity, justice, and love. The journal contains games, songs, devotional practices, and informal learning modules suitable for parents who want to be involved in the religious training of their children. It is sponsored and organized by the National Spiritual Assembly of the Baha'i of the United States.

CONTROVERSIES

As previously indicated, there was considerable controversy at the beginning of the Baha'i movement. The first leader, The Bab, was martyred, and two subsequent leaders were incarcerated for most or all of their lives. The Baha'is continue to cause controversy in those regions or nations in which they might be seen to challenge the religious hegemony of Islam. Baha'u'llah's claim that he was the Promised One of all religions can be seen as a direct challenge to the Islamic view that Muhammad is the Seal of the Prophets (the last or final Prophet). Baha'u'llah also sparked controversy when he claimed that all religions were equal, that men and women should be equal before the law as they are before God, and that slavery should be universally banned. None of these ideas were popular in the nineteenth century, either in the Middle East or in the United States. The Shah of Iran (Persia) exiled Baha'u'llah to destroy his movement. The Ottoman Empire kept him imprisoned to try to silence him. Nevertheless, his controversial ideas found an audience and the movement grew.

During the Iranian Revolution of 1978–1979, when the U.S.-backed government of Mohammad Reza Shah Pahlavi fell, many religious minority groups (Christian, Zoroastrian, Jewish, Druze, and Baha'i) were persecuted by the Ayatollah Khomeni's new government, which wanted to establish a sweeping, unified Shi'ah Islam within Iran. Many of the Baha'i emigrated from Iran at that time, principally to the United States, Europe, and India. Today, some 350,000 Baha'is remain in Iran. They are often subjected to discriminatory treatment in housing, jobs, and education. In 1996, the United Nations Commission on Human

Rights specifically mentioned the Baha'i (among others) in a statement calling for Iran to cease its persecution of religious minorities. Many spiritual and political leaders in Iran have accused the Baha'i in Iran of spying for other countries.

In India, the Baha'i are a minority presence that is, for the most part, respected. In the United States, the Baha'i community is numerically small but quite stable and has a good working infrastructure. The International Center of the worldwide Baha'i community is in Haifa, Israel, near the site where The Bab, Baha'u'llah, and Abdu'l-Baha are buried. The Baha'is have generally been able to maintain a good working relationship with the government of Israel.

There have been a number of controversies that have involved the greater Baha'i community in recent years. The status of gay and lesbian members is currently being debated. Whereas the American Baha'i community has been relatively tolerant of committed gay or lesbian couples, attempts by these couples to have their relationships officially acknowledged have met with stiff resistance in the Universal House of Justice. In some cases, they have been stripped of their membership status. Heterosexual couples who have been married in non-Baha'i ceremonies have also had their memberships rescinded.

The Universal House of Justice also instituted a kind of pre-publication censorship several decades ago in order to control the manner in which Baha'i material was disseminated and interpreted. Currently, the focus of such controls resides in the National Spiritual Assemblies, which are responsible for policing and reviewing all Baha'i publications before they are made public. Although the initial ruling was understood as a temporary measure, it has remained in effect.

Similarly, there has been some controversy surrounding the development of unofficial Baha'i mailing lists and e-mail list servers. The universal message of Baha'u'llah has always appealed to a percentage of individuals who may want to be on a mailing list or who develop their own interpretations of the message without actually becoming members of the Baha'i faith. Because such mailing lists are difficult to control, the Baha'i World Center has been particularly concerned with maintaining a certain amount of scrutiny about list servers. Some former members have charged that they have been threatened with shunning for not closing down such lists. There have also been instances where individuals have been expelled because they publicly criticized the church in some manner.

After Shoghi Effendi, The Guardian, died suddenly in 1957, some Baha'is began to break away from the main body of the Baha'i community as various individuals proclaimed themselves to be Shoghi's true successor. Some authorities count up to seven groups that now claim to be "true Baha'i," but officially, all who are not affiliated with the Universal House of Justice are considered covenant breakers. The danger of public fusing of the larger church of Baha'is and one of these smaller groups is probably the main reason for the attempts to censor and control mailing lists, list servers, and publications. The Universal House of Justice refers to recognized, "orthodox" Baha'i as the Baha'i World Faith. Among the better known of the unrecognized, or splinter groups is the Baha'i Under the Provisions of the Covenant, organized under Mason Remey. The group is headquartered in Missoula, Montana, and claims a membership approaching 150,000, although this is almost certainly an exaggeration. The Orthodox Baha'i Faith or Mother Baha'i Council follow the claimed guardianship of Joel Marangella. The Orthodox Baha'i Faith Under the Regency was founded by claimant Rex King. The Charles Mason Remey Society broke off from the Under the Provisions followers under the leadership of Donald Harvey and Francis Spataro.

The Baha'i electoral process to the National Assemblies has also been criticized. The process is not public, and no discussion about the candidates is permitted. As a result, there has been almost no change in the nine-member U.S. National Spiritual Assembly since 1961. Additionally, even though men and women are supposed to be equal, a provision was made that the nine representatives residing at the Universal House of Justice would be male. Many Baha'is, particularly in Europe and the United States, believe that such a setup actually prohibits the very kind of equality that Baha'u'llah was trying to promote.

IN THE WORLD TODAY

The Baha'is' international movement is well organized and stable, but it appears to be growing slowly, particularly because the concepts of unity are often difficult to articulate (the question of how unity is to be accomplished comes up a great deal). Nevertheless, the Baha'i emphasis on the need to solve religious and political conflict in ways that are not violent does seem to be a particularly relevant message during this time of renewed religious and political global turmoil. According to scholars who have tracked the movement, people tend to join the Baha'i faith during times of political and social tension, and this has certainly increased, at least in the United States, in the past five years. That being said, the Baha'is have generally grown about 3 to 5 percent per year. In the United States, that will put the number of Baha'is at about 150,000 by 2010. The Baha'is have developed an international organization that has withstood many tests; their message of hope, reconciliation, and unity is directed at all races and religions. Undoubtedly, many will find this message attractive during the current political and religious uncertainties that more than likely will continue into the near future.

4

The Foursquare Gospel: A Pentecostal Church

The needs of humanity have never changed,
their heartaches, their sorrows,
their bodily sufferings have never changed.
He is still a satisfying portion who can meet
and supply every need for every body and soul.
He is still Jesus, the same yesterday, today and forever.

—Aimee Semple McPherson,
sermon/tract "Divine Healing"

INTRODUCTION

Pentecostal churches are among the most successful of all twentieth-century American Christian movements, and the Foursquare Church is one of the most successful of these. Pentecostalism can be traced to the nineteenth-century "holiness" movement, a transdenominational religious impulse that initially emerged out of revivalist Methodism but soon took on a life of its own and influenced the development and founding of other church movements. Holiness churches, as they developed, emphasized *Christian Perfectionism* or "entire sanctification." They also embraced the idea of a *second baptism*, the baptism of the Holy Spirit, which leads to a bestowing of the gifts of the spirit (speaking in tongues, prophecy, healing) upon the faithful. Additionally, they embraced the concept of heart purity, a condition that is said to lead to the desire to be of service, healing others, and preaching the gospel. Many of these ideas had been present in Methodist revivalism since the time of John Wesley (1703–1791). The Holiness movement (which flourished from 1830 to 1850 and then again from 1866 to 1899) emphasized the baptism of the spirit and the gifts of the spirit but added various premillennialist interpretations of church history.

Holiness churches were noted for their willingness to preach to mixed groups as well as for the important role that women played in these churches as ministers and healers. Phoebe Palmer, a very influential Holiness preacher, is largely credited with developing the Holiness theology, which described the actions of the Holy Spirit during the second baptism. She also wrote the first essay defending the right and responsibility of women to act as ministers and preachers. By the end of the nineteenth century, some Holiness churches had developed into distinctive denominations in their own right.

Pentecostal churches can, therefore, be seen as direct inheritors of the Holiness movement, although there are also some important differences. Because of their links with Methodism, Holiness churches maintained a fairly standard Trinitarian Christian theology. Pentecostal churches, which have loose institutional ties, have varied in their interpretations of Christian theology, generally opting for more practical religious formulations that can be readily applied and are confirmed and affirmed by revelation. For example, in the Foursquare Church, the personal functions of the Holy Spirit and Jesus as Christ are essentially merged even though the Church affirms a basic Trinitarian theology. Other Pentecostal churches, such as the Apostolic Congress, go still further and baptize individuals only in the name of Jesus Christ. Most Pentecostal churches, however, retain an emphasis on Christian perfectionism and premillennialism. Pentecostal churches also tend to emphasize the second baptism and have generally adopted free form styles of worship.

When counting their new members, many Pentecostal churches will note members who have been "water baptized" and those who have gone on to receive "spirit baptism." Water baptism is considered a preliminary act of faith, essential, but not quite enough. Water baptism ensures salvation. Spirit baptism indicates to an individual what his or her role in the church is to become. It is an additional means of grace that functions rather like the sacrament of Confirmation in mainline liturgical churches. The proof of spirit baptism is a gift bestowed upon the individual: the ability to speak in revelation or prophecy, *glossolalia* (speaking in tongues), healing, etc.

Modern Pentecostalism in the United States began on January 1, 1901, in Topeka, Kansas, during a Bible school session led by Charles Fox Parham, a former Methodist minister and a holiness preacher. One of his students, Agnes Ozman, began speaking in tongues. Parham saw this as proof that the power of the Holy Spirit would enable new missionaries to preach the gospel in foreign lands without needing to learn the native languages of other cultures. This revived power of the Holy Spirit would enable the gospel to reach right around the world. Parham began preaching this message throughout the Midwest.

It was not until Parham journeyed to Texas and his message was seized upon by African American preacher William Joseph Seymour in Houston, Texas, in 1905, that Parham's ideas began to spread. Seymour took Parham's insights and message to Azusa Street in Los Angeles and held his own revival at the African Methodist Episcopal Church in 1906. The resulting revival, called the Asuza Street movement, forged a potent mixture of white holiness doctrine with African American worship, and modern Pentecostalism was born. From Asuza Street, Pentecostal preachers began to spread the movement throughout the rest of the country and even overseas. Many Holiness churches began to align themselves with the new movement.

Today there are many independent Pentecostal churches (such as The Pentecostal Holiness Church, Fire-Baptized Holiness Church, the Pentecostal Free-Will Baptist Church) and numerous Pentecostal associations (larger organizations—such as Assemblies of God, Full Faith Church of Love, and International Foursquare Church—the independent churches may join). Seymour is now recognized as one of the most important African American preachers in American history, and his efforts in Los Angeles provided the paradigm for Pentecostal churches to follow over the subsequent years. Overwhelmingly, and often against the times, Pentecostal churches in the twentieth century would stretch, challenge, and reform mainstream Christian cultural perceptions of gender, race, class, and worship styles.

FOUNDATIONS OF THE FOURSQUARE GOSPEL

Aimee Elizabeth Kennedy was born on a small Canadian farm in 1890. In high school, Aimee attended a revival service led by Robert Semple. Although Aimee described her faith at the time as being "cold and far from God," something about the service moved her, and three days after the revival, Aimee experienced what is called being "born again." She continued to attend revival services and became convinced that God had a special plan for her. When Robert Semple asked her to marry and accompany him to China to set up a mission, Aimee assumed that this adventure was her calling. The couple traveled to China, but Robert Semple died a month later, and Aimee was left alone in a strange country to care for a new baby daughter.

She returned to the United States, married a businessman named Harold McPherson, and had another child, a son. She tried to settle down into a normal life, but she felt that God was still calling her to a special purpose. During a near fatal illness, Aimee McPherson declared to God that if she recovered, she would answer that calling. She later said that her healing followed quickly.

Aimee McPherson began to hold her own revivals. She traveled incessantly, up and down the East Coast, to the West Coast, throughout the South, and, eventually, around the world. Reportedly, she would share a stage with wrestlers or conduct a revival in a wealthy part of town and then go to the African American parts of town and continue to share her message. She assisted Hispanic missions in Los Angeles and is said to have converted a family of Gypsies in Denver, Colorado. Some sources suggest that she even preached in front of some Ku Klux Klan members who later threw away their white robes of racism. She was particularly known for her messages of hope and healing rather than for "fire and brimstone" messages that focused on the fear of hell and damnation. After her own experiences with disease, death, and recovery, McPherson began to emphasize the power of Jesus to heal: physically, mentally, emotionally, and spiritually. To this end, she established a special prayer ministry for healing.

The Foursquare Church was named after a vision inspired McPherson to take the Bible verse Ezekiel 40:47 as a mandate for the establishment of her special evangelizing mission to the world. As she described it, *foursquare* is a term used in the Bible to denote the balanced, completed building of the Temple of the Lord, which describes a sturdy foundation and denotes a mission that is "equally balanced on all sides, established and enduring."[1] Because it faces all directions, it is complete. Moreover, she interpreted foursquare as representing four aspects of Jesus Christ as the Savior, The Baptizer with the Holy Spirit, The Healer, and The Soon-Coming King. This vision came to her during an especially intense revival in Oakland, California, in the summer of 1922. The sermon that she delivered describing her revelatory experience became famous; in it she described the "foursquare gospel" as that which is perfect for the body, soul, spirit, and eternity.

Within a year, McPherson's founding church, the Angelus Temple, was established in Los Angeles, California, and she began broadcasting her unique evangelical vision over the radio. At a time when women were supposed to be married housekeepers, Aimee Semple McPherson was one of the most recognized public personalities in the United States. She was the first woman in the United States to receive an FCC radio license and is considered to be one of the pioneer religious broadcasters in American history. The Angelus Temple became a model of the Pentecostal ministry. It is estimated that the church provided food for more than 1.5 million people during the Great Depression.

SCRIPTURE

All Pentecostal churches rely principally on the Protestant Bible, whether in its traditional King James translation or newer translations. Although the Bible is commonly held to be error free in its inspiration, Pentecostal biblical interpretation also relies on practical and often quite specific applications of text. Visions or personal revelations are thought to "illumine" messages in scripture that may otherwise be hidden. In this sense, the Bible is viewed as a prophetic text that is a source of constant revelation, and this feature is emphasized much more than the idea that the text must always be "literally true." This view has provided Pentecostal congregations with a flexible theological standard by which to mission to others. As Aimee Semple McPherson said, for Pentecostals, "all are called and all are welcomed." [2]

WORLDVIEW AND ORGANIZATION

McPherson's goal was to spread the "good news" of Jesus throughout the world. Her son Rolf assumed leadership of the church after McPherson's death in 1944. He served as president and chairman of the increasingly global Foursquare organization for forty-nine years. The church describes the period from

1958 to 1971 as a "fallow period," when membership slowed but the organizational structure of the church was established and strengthened. In 1974, a major outreach campaign was attempted and membership grew. Rolf retired from his leadership role in 1988, and the presidency has been passed on twice. The current president is Dr. Paul Risser.

The Foursquare Church adopted a modified Episcopalian structure. The head of the organization consists of a president, a board of directors (which includes the vice president, a Director of Missions, and various district representatives and presidential appointees). There is also a Foursquare Cabinet, which includes nine district supervisors, and an executive council. The International Corporate Offices contain three divisions: The Executive Division, which handles legal and financial matters and is overseen by the president; the National Church Division, which oversees the Foursquare organization in the United States; and Foursquare Offices International, which is responsible for mission work outside the United States. Religious programs for youth are directed through a program called Radiance Life.

Each church is part of a district that is overseen by a district supervisor. The number of churches in the United States alone continues to grow, and this has recently created the need for reorganization. Currently, churches in the United States are being reorganized into fifty smaller districts, each of which will be served by one of three Regional Administration Centers (RAC). Individual churches are led by appointed pastors (men or women) and membership-elected church councils. The pastor is chosen by District Supervisors and the Board of Directors, but local church councils have final approval. The pastor of a church cannot act unilaterally regarding legal or financial issues. The church council representing the membership of the church has final say over such matters.

Foursquare Pentecostal Christians state that they are particularly dedicated to the following values: 1) They want the Church to be like an extended family; 2) They want to do their part to spread the gospel that "Jesus Christ is the Same, Yesterday and

Today and Forever;" 3) They strive to embrace a middle-of-the-road theology that minimizes division and stresses practicality and unity in Christ; and 4) They want their churches to be individual and creative and, at the same time, consistent in the spirit expressed within.

WORSHIP

Pentecostal churches vary widely in their worship formats. Each congregation has great flexibility. Generally, the pastor is largely responsible for establishing worship style, although larger congregations may actually hire a program or choir director to operate in this capacity. Foursquare churches follow what might be considered a typical Pentecostal worship format. Music is always an important component of worship. Congregants are encouraged to clap, dance, sway, and otherwise "get into the spirit." Often, a particular song will continue for fifteen to twenty minutes. At some point, the pastor will deliver a message, with frequent interludes for prayers of healing or intercession. Midway through the service, the pastor generally conducts a brief Bible study. Congregants are encouraged to participate, and the conversation can be quite lively as different translations of the Bible are compared. During the "praising" segments, congregants with particular needs may be invited to address the congregation. Praying, speaking in tongues, or other forms of conversing in the spirit may follow spontaneously. It is all rather free form with the pastor encouraging and facilitating participation. McPherson seems to have desired to save people through hope of salvation rather than by fear of damnation, and Foursquare pastors are encouraged to follow her example by inspiring and exhorting congregants rather than by using fire and brimstone rhetoric to frighten them into faith. Often, Foursquare pastors speak of lightening burdens, healing, and reconciliation. They tend to stress that all are equal and one in Jesus. In fact, there seems to be little pressure to "become saved" although that is clearly the hope and intention of such ministries.

OUTREACH AND MISSIONS

From the beginning, McPherson sought to reach out to others with the promise of God's healing and comfort. The Temple Angelus, now the International Church of the Foursquare Gospel, committed its resources to providing food, various social services, and ministry training programs. McPherson also hoped for the day "when the sun would never set on the Foursquare Gospel,"[3] and her vision seems to have been realized. It is now one of the largest Pentecostal organizations in the world, and its official Website counts 4.1 million churchgoers in 141 countries, with about 38,000 individual churches worldwide. Following McPherson's death in 1944, the Foursquare Church joined with other Pentecostal organizations (the Church of God, the Open Bible Standard Church, and the Pentecostal Holiness Church) to form the Pentecostal Fellowship of North America (now Pentecostal/Charismatic Churches of North America). The purpose of this larger organization was to facilitate fellowship and sharing of resources among diverse Pentecostal organizations. Recently, a four-year undergraduate college, Life Pacific College, has been operating under Foursquare/ Pentecostal auspices to provide an educational opportunity for Pentecostal students to study in the religious environment of their choosing.

CULTURAL EXPRESSIONS

The International Foursquare Church has adopted an official insignia that sets it apart from other Pentecostal organizations. It is called the Foursquare Flag, and its design came to McPherson in a moment of inspiration in 1931. It is a visual representation of the four aspects of Jesus' ministry. At the bottom of the flag is a red stripe signifying Christ as Savior. The gold-yellow stripe represents the fire of the Holy Spirit as experienced in the Second Baptism. Above that is a blue stripe that represents Jesus in his aspect as Healer. The purple stripe at the top represents the color of royalty, a reminder that Christ shall return to rule the earth. In the top left-hand corner, the number four is inscribed within a square, representing the foundations of the Temple. These are surmounted by a cross and a picture of an open Bible. The flag is flown over new mission churches around the world, specifically identifying such missions as Foursquare.

CONTROVERSIES

McPherson's public life was often rife with controversy. First, she was a well-known public figure during a time when women were not supposed to be independent. Then, in May 1926, she disappeared while swimming at a public beach in Venice, California. The news media was swamped with speculations about kidnapping, illicit romantic affairs, and murder. When she reappeared at the end of June, she told a harrowing and rather spectacular story about having escaped a vicious kidnapping. Many in the media doubted her story was true; eventually she was charged with falsifying evidence and corrupting public morals. After several months of testimony, the district attorney assigned to the case finally dropped all charges against her in January 1927. There were several other attempts over the next decade to bring charges against McPherson. She added to her public notoriety in 1931 by marrying David Hutton, a singer at the Angelus Temple in Los Angeles. The Church frowned upon remarriage if a former spouse was still alive, and she lost a few members because of the union. Nevertheless, the Foursquare Church regained its reputation through the years of the Depression by assisting millions of people with food and shelter.

Mainstream Christian bodies have occasionally criticized Pentecostal Christians for what is sometimes perceived as an overly emotional worship styles and theological flexibility. Some Pentecostal-style preachers, such as Jimmy Swaggert and Jim and Tammy Bakker, have become televangelists. If such celebrities have personal failings (monetary or sexual indiscretions), the media often makes much of it, implying that all Pentecostals are hypocritical and self-righteous. Most Pentecostal-Foursquare preachers are not famous, however, and are simply concerned with carrying out of the vision of McPherson.

Indeed, most Foursquare Christians are regular people with jobs and families, and are seeking a more immediate experience of God in their lives. Occasionally they turn to the Church for specific reasons: unemployment, homelessness, loneliness, to cope with the illness of a family member, or to seek healing. Foursquare churches have oriented themselves to address these particular difficulties. This, more than anything else, is probably the reason for their continued growth and success.

Although there is evidence that McPherson ministered directly to African Americans and that many other Pentecostal churches have successful interracial communities, it is also true that some Pentecostal churches, particularly those in the South, have not always been able to overcome traditional social and racial divides. Despite the contributions of African Americans to Pentecostalism, many Pentecostal bodies have had significant difficulty with racial integration. This, at least in part, has led to the formation of exclusively African American Pentecostal Congregations. In April 1992, the International Church of the Foursquare Convention drafted a denominational statement that addressed racism and took a strong stand against any and all expressions of racial discrimination in the Church. The Church asked for collective forgiveness and expressed a strong commitment to fight racism in any and all manifestations: institutional, personal, social, and political.

IN THE WORLD TODAY

Pentecostalism has been extremely influential among mainstream American Christian bodies. In addition to the "classic Pentecostal" congregations, of which the Foursquare Church is one example, Pentecostal-*charismatic* styles of worship have been adopted and adapted by other church bodies to augment and develop their own worship styles. Catholic, Lutheran, Episcopalian, Methodist, and Disciples of Christ congregations have experimented with or adopted various aspects of Pentecostal worship in order to attract or keep congregants. African American churches, such as the African Methodist Episcopal

Church, have reintegrated aspects of Pentecostal worship into their services as well. Many of these congregations adopt Pentecostal-charismatic worship techniques or "move in signs and wonders," but retain the traditional theologies and features of their established worship services. Many mainstream Christians feel that Pentecostal-charismatic worship experiences provide valuable tools for spiritual growth. It is a testament to the perceived need of many Americans for a more intimate, personal experience of religious faith. As of 2001, the combined world membership of the International Foursquare Church was estimated at about 5 million people in 141 countries, with a total of about 38,000 churches. Foursquare Offices International predicts that these numbers will continue to rise as Pentecostal churches of all kinds continue to spread around the globe. May 2004 was designated a prayer initiative month, and members in all Foursquare churches were invited to pray together for the continued growth and health of the International Church. At this point, the continued growth and development of the Foursquare Church seems certain.

5

Raelians:
A UFO Religion

The future of humanity is in its own hands,
and the truth is in yours.
Communicate it throughout the world.

—Rael, The Message Given by Extraterrestrials

INTRODUCTION

UFO religions are singular, unique faiths that are fundamentally linked to human technological advances made in the last sixty years. Almost all of them can be traced to the UFO *contactee movement* of the 1950s, although some may reflect certain elements, such as spiritualism or theosophy, that go back to the late nineteenth century.[4] Throughout the 1950s and 1960s, various individuals such as George Adamski, George Van Tassel, Howard Menger, Daniel Fry, George King, and Wallace C. Halsey, claimed to have had contact with extraterrestrial beings. The cosmic visitors warned these contactees about the abuses of science and technology, frequently uttered prophecies of impending doom, and often provided reinterpretations of traditional biblical stories. The development of weapons of mass destruction, particularly atomic weaponry such as that used on the Japanese city of Hiroshima, signaled a new, potentially terminal age for humanity. Contactees began to advocate controls on such technologies, warning that humanity could be wiped out if care was not taken. Often, the extraterrestrials were said to be warning humans not to make the kinds of mistakes that had plagued their own civilizations.

Not all of the contactees went on to create UFO religious movements, but many of their stories and prophecies, such as Adamski's and Fry's warnings about the dangers of nuclear weapons and radiation, were incorporated into an expanding narrative of potential human self-annihilation. Van Tassel's Ashtar Command spawned a network of autonomous religious groups all claiming contact with the same benevolent extraterrestrial groups. King's Aetherius Society has the distinction of being one of the oldest ongoing UFO religious groups. Halsey helped found a group called Christ Brotherhood and reportedly mysteriously vanished while on a plane headed to Nevada in 1963. A UFO group first founded in 1975, Heaven's Gate gained international notoriety when most of the membership committed mass suicide in 1997, in the belief they would be taken aboard a space ship that was signaled by the approach of the Hale-Bopp comet.

The Raelians (pronounced Ri-lee-ans), founded in 1975, constitute the largest organized international UFO religious group in the world. Membership numbers range from forty thousand to sixty thousand (depending on the source) and members live in eighty-four to ninety countries. The highest membership concentration is found in the United States, the Canadian province of Quebec, France, and Japan; additional members are scattered throughout Europe, South Africa, and South America. The founder of the group, Claude Vorilhon, claims to have had contact with an extraterrestrial that came to Earth in a flying saucer (UFO). Vorilhon says he was chosen as a prophet because he was born after the destruction of the Japanese city of Hiroshima by atomic weapons in 1945. Raelians seek to dismantle atomic weaponry and all other methods of mass destruction.

The Raelian religion is quite unique in that it also promotes what it calls an atheistic and scientific view that is nonetheless intimately tied to biblical interpretation. Furthermore, unlike many other UFO religious groups, Raelians have openly and enthusiastically embraced nonlethal technology and science, asserting that human beings simply need to learn how to utilize technology responsibly for the betterment, rather than the destruction of life. To this end, Raelians strongly support new biogenetic research, including cloning, DNA coding, and stem-cell research. They view these technologies as supportive of evolving human life. At the same time, Raelians distance themselves from other UFO religious groups. They tend to be doubtful of the claims of other contactees or UFO abductees. Their unique views make the Raelians a fascinating and contro-versial New Religious Movement.

FOUNDATIONS

According to the Raelian foundation story, Claude Vorilhon, a struggling French journalist and occasional racecar driver, was contacted by an extraterrestrial while visiting an extinct volcano near the French village of Clermont-Ferrand on December 13, 1973. The extraterrestrial descended in a small bell-shaped UFO that first appeared as a flashing red light and was completely silent. The extraterrestrial that disembarked from the ship was about four feet tall, "with pale green skin, almond-shaped eyes, and long dark hair."[5] The extraterrestrial spoke to Vorilhon in perfect French and, after a bit of small talk, revealed to Vorilhon that he had been chosen to write down and relay a message to humanity from its creators. Vorilhon met with the extraterrestrial for the next five days. The essence of the message that Vorilhon was to deliver to humanity is contained in his first book The Final Message (now entitled The Message Given by Extraterrestrials) and is summarized below.

The extraterrestrial explained that humans are genetically engineered creations, developed in off-world laboratories by a superior species called Elohim. The extraterrestrial identified itself as an Eloha (singular form of Elohim). According to Vorilhon (who was renamed Rael by the Eloha), the term Elohim, which appears in the Bible, has been consistently mistranslated and really means: "those who came from the sky."

Rael was told that the Elohim had become concerned about the destructive course that their most precious creation, humanity, had taken. They desired contact with humans in order to help. The Eloha revealed to Rael that the Elohim are

ELOHIM

The term Elohim is the Hebrew equivalent of Allah, one of the many Hebrew words in the Jewish Bible/Old Testament for the Divine or God. There is no one Jewish word for God. Elohim is grammatically plural and contains both male and female word elements. Some scholars have said that Elohim could more accurately be translated as Father-Mother "divine" Beings. Still, in standard English translations of Elohim, the simple singular of "God" is used. Rael's reported retranslation of the term is definitely nonstandard.

humanity's physical and genetic creators and have also helped to create and fashion the great religions of humanity in an attempt to encourage the growth of humanitarianism and good government. To facilitate the contact process, and also demonstrate the goodwill of human beings toward their galactic parents, Rael was told to build an embassy in Jerusalem, Israel, and to continue spreading the truth about human origins.

The basis for the Raelian claim of atheism comes from Rael's report of the Eloha's contention that the divine beings of all earthly religions are based on misunderstandings of the nature of the true creators of humanity. There is no God in the monotheistic sense. The Elohim are not gods, they are simply a superior life-form that enjoys genetically creating life in the same fashion that an artist expresses himself in painting, writing, or composing. Humans are special because they are the creatures that the Elohim created most like themselves or in their own image.

SCRIPTURES

Rael has authored several books in which he reveals the ongoing messages of the Elohim. Although Raelians do not necessarily believe that Rael is the only individual that the Elohim could contact, they maintain that Rael is the prophet of this age and, for this reason, only contact with him is above suspicion. Some Raelians report that they feel they may be in contact with the Elohim directly during some of their *Sensual Meditation* practices, but none of them would declare themselves to be communicating with the Elohim in the same manner that Rael is said to have done. Rael's first book, The Final Message, details his initial contact with the Elohim, his journeys to their planet, and the true interpretation of the Bible and human history, which they provided for him to reveal in subsequent writings. Together these writings comprise aspects of the Raelian mission.

Yes to Human Cloning expresses how the Elohim explained to Rael the real basis for human immortality in the scientific practices of biotechnology and genetic science. There is no soul outside the body, but biotechnology will allow for the

gradual perfection of the human body. The unique characteristics of each individual can be continuously "downloaded"
over time into subsequent cloned and perfected bodies. Each
individual will accumulate the life experiences of many embodi-
ments and will eventually achieve both physical immortality
and godly wisdom. Let's Welcome the Extraterrestrials explains
the necessity of building an embassy to welcome the Elohim.
Once this embassy is built, the Elohim can safely come to Earth
and contact their creation, humanity. Finally, Sensual Meditation
explains the basic religious practices of the Raelian seminars.
All of these texts are considered to be scriptural, reflecting and
transmitting the words and teachings of the Elohim through
the utterances of Rael.

According to the Raelian Website, the purpose of these writings
is to demystify traditional religion by providing a more technological, scientific understanding of orthodox religious belief
and practice while, at the same time, spiritualizing earthly life
and encouraging individuals to see the spiritual and religious
aspects of technology and human material development. The
writings of Rael are said to correct the errors that developed
in more traditional religious writings, such as the Bible and
the Koran.

WORLDVIEW AND ORGANIZATION

Raelians maintain that all world religions were originally
founded by the Elohim. All world religions, furthermore, have
developed a distorted image of the creators of humanity, seeing
them as divine rather than simply technologically superior
beings. The great religious teachers such as Moses, Jesus,
Buddha, Muhammad, and even Joseph Smith are understood
by Raelians to have been human-Elohim genetic hybrids. Rael
has claimed that, just as the great prophetic figures of old were
genetic hybrids, he himself is the product of a mother impreg-
nated by an Eloha (extraterrestrial).

As a result, all holy books and all religions have a kernel of
truth, but all have been distorted by teachings of guilt and control.

As The Final Message puts it: "Traces of this epic master-piece of creation [the genetic project of the Elohim to create humanity] can be found in all religious writings. It would take many pages to name all the religions and sects that testify in a more or less obscure way to our work."[6] Rael is considered the last of these hybrid teachers, and he has been chosen to reveal to humanity the final truth. This revelation is now possible because humans have attained the technological prowess to be able to understand the reality of their own genetic creation and can eventually progress to the point where they could become like the Elohim themselves by improving upon and creating new forms of life.

To facilitate and spread this vision, the Raelian movement has adopted a hierarchical organization, called The Structure, that is intended to organize, systematize, and disseminate Rael's teachings. Raelians frequently summarize their beliefs by citing the three official aims of The Structure:

- To inform without convincing

- To establish the embassy

- To catalyze a society adapted to the future

A recent book by Susan Palmer, *Aliens Adored: Rael's UFO Religion*, provides the first systematic study of the Raelian movement. Her description of The Structure indicates that the Raelian hierarchy consists of the following levels: Probationer (new member), Assistant Animator, Animator, Assistant Guide, Priest Guide, Bishop Guide, and Planetary Guide. It is known that the transmission ritual (described on the following page) is generally conducted by Priest Guides. The various guides also organize and lead activities at the Yearly Seminars. Some specialize in teaching certain techniques of Sensual Meditation. As of 2002, there were an estimated 130 Priest Guides worldwide. Academic literature still does not describe the precise functions of the other levels, although some are presumably training levels.

Raelians emphasize that their organization runs entirely by tithing, and it is true that at the entry level all Raelian events are free. Advanced training seminars that may lead to higher placement within The Structure can be quite costly, however, although not everyone is expected to be able to pay for and attend such sessions. Individuals pay for the advancement that they desire and can afford. Although the prophetic figure of Rael is revered by many Raelians, he often attempts to maintain a fairly low public profile. His leadership style is generally described as nonauthoritarian. Although he does not allow political rivals to emerge within his organization, he also does not seem to vilify individuals who choose to leave. Criticism of Raelians has generally focused on specific aspects of their religious belief and practice rather than charges of brainwashing or monetary exploitation.

WORSHIP

There are two principal ceremonies unique to Raelians. The *transmission of the cellular code* operates as a baptism and initiation, and is generally administered to new members by Priest Guides, individuals who have reached a relatively high level in The Structure. The transmission generally involves close physical contact between the Guide and the Probationer: the laying of hands on the head and neck or even a full body hug have been reported. Much of the transmission is mental, although certain guides intone what seems to be a word formula as a kind of blessing on the occasion. The transmission is regarded as a kind of rudimentary reprogramming that reawakens the genetic memory of the Elohim in a probationer's DNA. Because Raelians believe that perfection of the human physical body is possible, indeed vital, for the development of one's true mental and spiritual potential, the transmission is considered a precursor of perfection.

The second principal ceremonial activity that is unique to the Raelian movement is Sensual Meditation, a group activity that typically takes place during Yearly Seminars. The principles of Sensual Meditation are often stated in the following manner:

- Happiness is our natural state.

- Fear switches off higher consciousness and turns us into obedient, malleable citizens.

- Human civilization is in a transition period in which one foot is stuck in the old world of fear and one foot is stuck in the new world of endless possibility and progression.

- Sensuality (meaning complete physical, sensual awareness) is the solution.

Raelian Sensual Meditation has evolved over the years into a rather complex series of visualization and meditation practices occurring at the individual and group level. These practices are intended to break down all cultural barriers inhibiting an individual's total personal, sexual, and emotional expression. Generally, the Sensual Meditation itself begins with a fairly elaborate visualization that focuses on the body and is sometimes referred to as "oxygenation." The individual is encouraged to visualize all the organs in the body separately, to imagine the body being taken apart piece by piece. Once the individual has fully experienced this disassembling of the body components, he or she visualizes the body being put back together again. The Yearly Seminar offers training sessions in group Sensual Meditation to welcome new members and for workshops that teach Raelians to integrate positively the principles of Rael into their personal and professional lives. Participants are given plenty of free time during seminars to explore their personal and sexual connections with one another. Raelians emphasize that most social taboos limiting human sexual expression are oppressive and demeaning. As a result, for adults, most forms of human sexual expression, including bi-, trans-, and homosexuality, are encouraged and accepted in the Raelian community. Many Raelians are quite open about their sexual practices and often eager to pursue sexual contact with other members.

This has led to the charge that Raelians encourage sexual deviance and that the Seminars are simply excuses for orgies, a charge that evidence does not support. Although Raelians might hold unconventional views about human sexual expression, their activities are not coercive. No one is expected to engage in sexual activities that are personally distasteful (or even engage in them at all). It should be noted here that many Raelians are in stable heterosexual marriages. Moreover, Raelians are very strict about adult consent. Of all the sexual charges of which the Raelians have been accused, it appears that no one has ever accused the group of engaging in or encouraging the sexual abuse of children. At the same time, Raelians are vigorous supporters of responsible sexual expression, birth control, and abortion rights. They have often riled local school boards in Montreal, Canada, by passing out free condoms to Catholic high school students. Raelians have become regular participants in Gay Pride events and AIDS rallies.

GROWING UP

Occasionally, Raelians have been accused of having ambiguous feelings about family and children. This seems to be related to statements that Rael has made about abortion, birth control, and adult responsibility. He has, from time to time, implied that women who have become pregnant or women who actually bear children and then realize that they really do not want to have or rear children should be allowed easy abortions or ready access to adoption facilities. "Thus, if you gave birth to the child you desired . . . and you no longer desire the child, you will be able to entrust him to society so that he may be brought up in harmony necessary for his fulfillment."[7] In context, his comments appear to focus on the dilemma of what it means to be an unwanted child. He thinks it preferable that a child be aborted or adopted rather than be brought up in a home where the mother resents the child's existence and could do the child great psychological harm. Rael's emphasis here seems to be that only adults who can responsibly raise children should be allowed to do so.

Rael seems to advocate a form of eugenics in which only adults who can be said to be "superior" should be allowed to reproduce or act in positions of political leadership. At the same time, Rael does seem to be aware of how his position of *geniocracy* (rule by the genetically fit) might be interpreted, so he does not advocate the elimination of "inferiors." According to this logic, with applied biotechnology, there will eventually be no inferiors.

Although the Raelian religion seems to be principally aimed at adults, the numbers of Raelian families with children has been increasing. This shift is being addressed at the seminar level in which simplified Sensual Meditation techniques are taught to the young. Although data on Raelian children are very sparse, a second generation of Raelians is emerging, and it is hoped and expected that more information on child rearing may be forthcoming. Furthermore, the Raelian interest in cloning and other reproductive technologies virtually insures that the organization is at least psychologically investing in the idea of future generations.

CULTURAL EXPRESSIONS

As previously mentioned, one of the primary goals of the Raelian movement is the establishment and construction of an embassy for the Elohim in Israel, preferably Jerusalem. According to Rael, the idea for the embassy was transmitted to him quite early in his initial contact with the Elohim. He contends that by contacting humanity in Israel, the Elohim intend to literally and materially fulfill biblical expectations of the coming of the messiah, or the Mahdi, as hoped for by many Jewish, Christian, and Muslim peoples. The only surprise for orthodox believers will be the spaceships. The Raelians have reportedly raised over $7 million for this project, and the government of Israel has been contacted directly numerous times for permission to build the embassy. To date, all petitions have been denied or ignored.

For a time, many observers maintained that the Raelian medallion could have been one of the reasons for the lack of

Israeli enthusiasm for the project. The original design featured a swastika inscribed within a six-pointed star. This combination of a former Nazi symbol with a symbol that is now used to designate the state of Israel was considered by many to be an affront to the people of Israel. The symbol was changed in 1990 with the permission of the Elohim. It now consists of a six-pointed star emerging from an abstract swirling galaxy. The changing of the symbol has not made the Israeli government any more responsive to Raelian requests.

The Raelians have constructed a UFO-inspired theme park, which is located near Montreal, Canada. The theme park, which opened in August 1997, boasts the largest building in the world constructed of processed hay bales. It contains exhibits featuring the true history of humanity as revealed to Rael by the Elohim. Visitors can also see a replica of the spaceship used by the Elohim and a twenty-six-foot sculpture of the human DNA molecule.

CALENDAR AND HOLIDAYS

Researchers know very little about Raelian holidays, partly because most Raelians seem very individualistic about the holidays they choose to observe. Personal birthdays and selected national or religious holidays may be observed. The most important official event in the Raelian calendar is the Yearly Seminar. Generally, only one of these is held each year on those continents in which Raelians have a large enough presence to make such an event financially feasible. Yearly Seminars make it possible for Raelians to meet, practice group Sensual Meditation, receive training, and be initiated or ordained into higher levels of The Structure. Rael often makes surprise appearances at the Yearly Seminars.

Rael frequently makes official pronouncements about the year to come, setting the theme of the year for The Structure. For example, 2004 was declared the Year of Atheism. This theme has been taken up in the Raelian newsletter in which Rael and other Structure authorities have spent a great deal of time linking the belief in God to fanaticism and terrorism. Along the same lines, in June 2004, Rael issued a press release offering spiritual sanctuary to members of the U.S. Congress who might be denied communion because of their views on gay marriage or abortion rights. He declared that since these members of Congress are being accused of apostasy anyway, they might as well just admit it and become Raelians.

The proclaimed annual theme also becomes a focus for activities of the Yearly Seminar. There seem to be no officially designated days that celebrate Rael's ascension as a prophet of the Elohim or Rael's person, but this situation may change as Rael ages and the issue of succession emerges.

CONTROVERSIES

Raelians have distinguished themselves more than once in the public arena by adopting many social and political positions that are quite controversial. Indeed, Rael is quoted as having said, "Conformism is the opposite of intelligence."[8] The controversies attending Raelian views regarding human sexual expression and traditional religious theologies have already been noted. Perhaps no issue has thrust them into public scrutiny more than the 2002 public announcement made by the Raelian genetics company, Clonaid. The announcement boasted that Raelian scientists had succeeded in cloning a human embryo and that the embryo was being carried by a prospective parent. It aroused a great deal of media interest and scientific skepticism. The claims of Clonaid scientists have not been confirmed by outside experts, but the Clonaid Website explains the purpose for the development of cloning technology as a scientific technique that will eventually result in genetic perfection of the human species and physical immortality. Because Raelians believe that all emotional, mental and spiritual aspects of humanity are ultimately genetic in origin, such an idea is consistent with their teachings. Cloning is simply in keeping with the overall nature of human evolution, which itself originated in a genetic experiment conducted by the Elohim.

According to Rael, cloning technology will enable couples who cannot conceive, including infertile and homosexual couples, to reproduce by using their own genetic material. Families who have lost children or other loved ones can get them back through the process of cloning. Individuals who have diseases can reproduce without passing on their ailments to offspring. Pets can be restored to their owners. These are among the many human needs and services that Clonaid seeks to address. The social and political issues that the Raelians have raised can be seen in the role that Rael played when he was asked to testify before the U.S. House Subcommittee on Oversight and Investigations on March 28, 2001. At the subcommittee hearing regarding "Issues Raised by Human Cloning Research," Rael testified on behalf of Clonaid.

Raelian emphasis on physical perfection has also led to strong criticism of Rael's perceived lack of compassion for physically or mentally handicapped individuals. Rael has made statements that clearly indicate his personal belief that only leaders who are deemed "genetically fit" should be allowed to lead—and this necessarily precludes individuals who are born with congenital deformities or handicaps. (There is no evidence that he includes individuals who have been damaged by accident or subsequent illness.) At the same time, Raelians strongly support any and all research that seeks to uncover and prevent the causes of genetic deformity. One of the stated purposes of Clonaid is to use genetic research to discover means by which individuals who may have been mentally or physically compromised by accident, illness, or genetic mutation can be healed of their infirmities. Thus, rather than "eliminating" such individuals, Raelians desire to "correct" the physical reasons for their "inferiority." In this way, properly applied biotechnology can serve as a kind of physical salvation for individuals, whereas, in the past, physical perfection and salvation had to wait for an afterlife.

IN THE WORLD TODAY

While it is not clear how quickly the Raelian religion will grow in the coming years, it is abundantly clear that the issues of human sexuality and biotechnology, which Raelians address, will continue to be hotly debated. This alone will probably keep Raelians in the news from time to time. It may, in fact, periodically attract new members. There seems to be a growing emphasis in Raelian literature on focusing the message of the Elohim specifically to populations that may benefit from or be encouraged by the openness of Raelians to diverse sexual expression and biotechnological development: for example, gays or people with incurable diseases. Rael has recently published new information in which he has openly declared himself to be Maitreya and the Mahdi (Buddhist and Muslim "promised ones"). The Structure seems to be reorganizing for extended mission work and preparing for the reality of succession. It is to be expected that The Structure will continue to develop and refine Sensual Meditation techniques and the message of the Elohim. As noted, Raelians are quite unique in their adamant defense of the possibilities of human technological achievement. If nothing else, they seem to have struck a nerve by correctly identifying several converging issues (technology, biogenetics, and human sexual diversity) facing human civilization. That they have taken a position on these concerns is not surprising. The Raelians seem to be poised to continue challenging traditional religious and social perceptions. It remains to be seen how the nations of the world tackle the same issues.

6

Orisha Worship: Ifa, Santeria, Candomble, and Lukumi

Mo dupe Ori Egun, ase.
I give thanks for the wisdom of the ancestors,
May it be so.

—Traditional Yoruban ending for Ancestor Altar installation,
Translation by Awo Fa'lokun Fatunmbi

INTRODUCTION

The term *Orisha worship* generally describes a complex of practices that originated in what is now Nigeria, Africa, among an ancient people who still call themselves the *Yoruba*. The term *Ifa* is used primarily by the Yoruba to describe their traditional religious practice of forging long-term and complex relationships with ancestral beings and personified natural forces referred to as *Orishas*. The Yoruba people were among those Africans taken into slavery to be sold in the Americas from the sixteenth to the nineteenth centuries. Many retained their traditional beliefs despite attempts to convert them to Christianity. Often, elements of Christianity were simply incorporated into Yoruban beliefs. Depending on where the Yoruba were taken, different variations of Orisha worship developed.

In Brazil, Orisha worship combined with elements of native Indian and Catholic practice and is now called Candomble, a variation that claims millions of followers in Brazil alone. Candomble was established as a recognized religion in Brazil in the 1930s and is centered in Bahia, Brazil. Cuban and other Caribbean practitioners will often refer to their religion as Santeria, and their Orishas are called "santos" or saints. Santeria developed in the mid-nineteenth century and is often distinguished by a tight identification of the Orishas with Catholic saints. Candomble practitioners often deny any significant Catholic identification.

Orisha worshippers in the United States practice Lukumi or Santeria (particularly in Cuban communities). Recently, they have started to use the term Ifa to refer to their religion, and occasionally will use Ifa and Lukumi interchangeably. Practitioners of Santeria often use the terms Lukumi, La Regla Lakumi, or Regla de Ocha when speaking of their religion, with Santeria being the most popular.

In all cases, in each location and variation, many elements of Orisha worship have remained the same. There is a core group of Orishas who are most frequently called upon and venerated. The basis of the religion is oral and initiatory, and the primary practices of worship involve chanting, dancing, possession, or "being ridden" by one's principal Orisha. Ritual animal sacrifice and feasting are part of initiation and ceremony, and there is periodic engagement in rituals that, in the West, are probably classified as "magic(k)al." In the remainder of this chapter, Ifa will be used to explain Orisha worship generally; for descriptions of specific Santerian or Candomble practices, the terms Santeria or Candomble will be used.

A distinction between Orisha worship and practices referred to as *Vodu, Umbanda, Quimbanda, Palo Myombe,* or *Macumba* needs to be made. Vodu, Umbanda, Palo Myombe, and Quimbanda are religious systems that, like Ifa, also emerged from African groups who were forcibly brought to the Americas as slaves. Vodu originated in the beliefs and practices of the Dahomeyan, Fon, and Congolese peoples and is now found primarily in Caribbean countries such as Haiti. Umbanda and Quimbanda developed from other African groups and are practiced primarily in South America. *Macumba* is a term that is frequently used in a negative fashion to describe Santerian practitioners in the same fashion that the term *voodoo* has come to describe Vodu believers. Vodu means "the divinities" or "that which is divine"; Vodu believers forge relationships with beings called *loa,* and there are some similarities between loa and Orishas. Many of the practices of Vodu, Umbanda, and Quimbanda are similar and include dancing, chanting, and ritual possession. The content of chanting and ritual in each of the religions, however, is quite distinct, although they share some common African ritual techniques.

In all Orisha systems, the Yoruban language is regarded as a sacred key used to contact the spiritual force of the Orishas. Great effort is made to preserve Yoruban word forms and traditional chants, regardless of whether a practitioner's native tongue is Spanish, English, or Portuguese. Nonetheless, there are numerous practitioners who have become "fluent" in multiple African-based religions, and it is not uncommon to find these followers performing Candomble one day and Umbanda the next or for a Santerian or Lukumi priest to invoke a loa. Such overlap has made it difficult for Western academics to completely define or categorize all aspects of these African-based faiths. These faiths are living, growing, and expanding systems with tens of millions of worshippers worldwide. What began as a traditional belief system common to a particular tribal or ethnic group is developing with astonishing rapidity into a complex world religion.

FOUNDATIONS

All Orisha worshippers believe that the cosmos and the planet ultimately came from one source, one creator called Oludumare (pronounced Oh-lood-oo-mah-ray). This single source gave birth to the powers that create and run the forces of nature on Earth. Foremost among the powers that created humankind is the Orisha, Obatala. He is considered the chief Orisha, the father, the one to whom all the other Orishas defer. For Orisha worshippers, the world-cosmos is full of energy, and there is no essential difference or division between the physical and spiritual worlds. The energy that circulates throughout all realms containing the power of creation is called *ache* or *ashe* (ah-chay or ah-shay).

Beings in both the physical and spiritual realms are classified in several categories: There are the Orishas, the *Eguns* (ancestors), humans, and other beings (plants, animals, rocks, etc). In Ifa, everything is alive in some way; true death is an illusion. Souls can be lost, trapped, or refound, but true death is impossible. The spiritual world is simply another way of existing, and it is continuous with the physical world. The Orishas are beings that serve as intermediaries between the celestial realm of Oludumare and humans—rather like angels or saints might in Roman Catholicism. Although they are immortal, they are neither all-powerful nor perfect.

The Eguns can be relatives who have passed from the physical realm, individuals who act as spiritual ancestors or teachers, or people who have been inspirational, such as a philosopher whose teachings an individual admires. Finally, the Eguns can be reincarnational relatives, those to whom one is related in larger collective family groups. In Ifa, the Eguns are constantly attempting to relate to those still living as they continue to express desires and influence descendants. They must be acknowledged and respected.

Humans operate in a special capacity. They must seek out the knowledge of all the other realms, and to some degree, they are the moral pivot on which the world turns. Because humans have choices that Orishas and Eguns do not, they can actively change the world in specific ways. A Yoruban saying puts it this way: "Except for the day of birth and the day of death, there is nothing else that humans cannot change." Both the Orishas and the Eguns are dependent on humans for feeding and remembering them. Humans help to maintain a kind of natural flow for the ache. Finally, there is the power of plants, animals, rocks, and other natural forces or beings. Each of these has a story, a power, or a remedy to share with humans, and humans are expected to learn and use these stories and remedies. When the relationship between humans and these other realms becomes unbalanced, sickness or discord results. It is up to humans to discover the nature of the imbalance and seek the remedy.

Some Orishas represent forces of nature such as lightning and thunder, rivers, the ocean, powers of plants, and the earth. Others are understood to have originally been Eguns, or particular ancestors, who through great deeds or great ache (power) were elevated to the status of Orisha. Traditional Ifa claims that there are 401 Orishas. Most practitioners and worshippers are familiar with approximately twenty principal Orishas. Popular references often reduce the number of principal Orishas to seven or eight. The most commonly mentioned Orishas include Obatala, Ogun, Oya, Oshun (Erzulie), Elegba/Eshu, Chango (Xango Shango), Yemaya (Yemoja), and Ochosi (Oxosi).

Each Orisha is associated with particular colors, foods, songs, and objects through which a practitioner offers prayers and praise. For example, Oshun (Oxun, Ossain), the Orisha of rivers, is signified by the colors orange, gold, and yellow. Her favorite foods include honey, pumpkinseeds, and oranges, and there are specific songs that sing her praises. She is very beautiful, maybe a little vain, and is associated with mirrors, hand fans, and other objects of beauty. Her day is either Thursday or Friday, and her number is five. Although she is considered the Orisha of love, she can also be consulted for assistance with war and conflict. To contact her, an individual must first consult an *Awo* or *Santero*; he or she may then offer gifts of food, yellow candles, or other objects Oshun favors. Devotees of Oshun keep an altar to her in their homes, "feeding" it periodically. (For a list of the Orishas and what they are associated with, see the table on the following page.)

Some Orishas are male and others female, but their sex does not determine which humans they choose. (Orishas choose their humans, not the other way around). Whereas Ogun and Chango, both male warrior Orishas, can be the patrons of women, Oshun, the goddess of love, frequently chooses men. Some Orishas, such as Obatala, Ellegua, and Chango, change their sex from time to time, which might be confusing to humans but is apparently not difficult for Orishas.

WORLDVIEW AND ORGANIZATION

There is a ritual hierarchy that Orisha worshippers access by initiation and attainment. The most basic level is that of the worshipper. A worshipper has had assistance in determining his or her ruling Orisha and attends ritual festivals. At such festivals, it is easy to tell which Orisha rules each worshipper by the *ileke* or Orisha beads he or she wears. Each Orisha is symbolized by specific colors and beaded patterns. When a worshipper goes into trance and is "mounted" by the Orisha, it is understood that the Orisha enters into or uses the physical vehicle of the worshipper. If a worshipper requires specific assistance, he or she may consult an Awo or a Santero (in Cuba) who will perform divination to assist in determining the nature of the imbalance. Once the nature of the difficulty is ascertained, the worshipper is given *Ebbo* or a work or ritual to perform to

ORISHA CORRESPONDENCE TABLE

ORISHA	COLORS	SYMBOL	POWER	NUMBER	DAY	FOOD	SAINT
Obatala	White	White Cloth of Peace	Peace/ Father/ Leader	8	Sunday	Rice/ Potatoe/ White food	Our Lady of Mercy
Ogun	Green/ Black	Stone/ Iron tools	War/ Healing/ Hermit	3 or 4	Tuesday	Nuts/Dried fruit/Meat/ Gin	Saint Peter
Chango	Red/ White	Double-bladed ax/ Thunder	Protect/ Warrior/ Defense/ Justice	6	Thursday/ Friday	Apples/ Rum/ Bananas/ Palm Oil	Saint Barbara
Oya	Purple/ White/ Black/ Rainbow	Horse tail whisk/ Whirlwind	Cemetary/ Market-place	9	Wednesday	Red Wine/ Eggplant	Saint Theresa
Oshun	Yellow/ Gold/ Orange	Rivers/ Mirrors/ Peacock feathers	Sex/ Love/ War/ Beauty	5	Friday	Honey/ Pumpkins/ Oranges	Our Lady of Caridad de Cobre
Ellegua	Red/ Black	Coconut Eye/ Head	Gate-Keeper/ Doors	3	Monday	Candy/Rum/ Cigars/ Toys	Saint Anthony of Padua
Yemaya	Blue/ White	Ocean	Fertility/ Family	7	Saturday	Corn Meal/ Pineapple/ Cane syrup	Our Lady of Regla
Ochosi	Dark Blue/ Orange	Bow and arrow	Hunting/ Fishing	7	Tuesday/ Thursday/ Saturday	Honey/ Game animals	Saint Norbert

set the balance right and affect the healing or resolve the conflict. The Ebbo generally consists of some kind of offering (in traditional communities, this can include animal sacrifice), songs, and prayers repeated over specific time periods.

Worshippers can choose to train as specialists in certain areas of healing or priestcraft. Some train to play *bata drums*, a specific kind of double-headed drum that is used in Yoruba-Ifa ceremonies and accompanies the *oriki* and *orin* or the traditional songs and poems of praise used to invoke the appearance of Orishas in their followers. Some learn to master the arts of herbcraft, Ase Ewe Orisha. One who becomes proficient at many of these crafts, divination, healing, and leading rituals, may eventually become a *Babalawo* a "father of secrets." In traditional Yoruban society, only men generally advance to this level. At each level (worshipper, Awo, or Babalawo), there is training, initiation, and testing. At the same time, this structure has been traditionally flexible and subject to a variety of checks and balances. For example, even though the Babalawo can perform any of the divinations, he cannot perform particular rituals, specifically some that relate to women. Women can perform as Awo, and in traditional Ifa societies, there are women priestesses and societies that are as powerful as men in rendering decisions that affect the entire group.

The political and religious structures exhibited by traditional Yoruban societies developed over many generations, and its export to the Americas has resulted in some variation. In many Santerian societies, the Santero may perform all the functions of an Awo and Babalawo. Individual Awo can become quite powerful in the West because they are far from the Nigerian village of Ile-Ife, the traditional center of Ifa. Some Western Awo have made the journey to Nigeria for traditional initiations; others have not. Some Awo have begun to alter many specific practices in order to accommodate Western attitudes toward divination and animal sacrifice. For example, Philip Niemark, an American who has accepted traditional Yoruban initiation, has established what he calls an American Ifa, which does not depend on the leadership of a Babalawo or on animal sacrifices. Niemark argues that the Orishas, as living entities, evolve in the same fashion that humans evolve. One need not sacrifice animals to them nor be overly dependent on traditional hierarchical forms of priestcraft. He cites specific instances in Yoruban history when the Orishas allowed their followers to forego such traditions. By doing so, he is following the example of many Cuban Santeros who have been interpreting Ifa in the same manner for over one hundred years. The practice has caused some controversy.

Communities such as the Kingdom of Oyotunji in Sheldon, South Carolina, and the Church of Lukumi Babalu Aye in Hialeah, Florida, attempt to retain and reinvigorate traditional Yoruban practices in the United States. Santerian and Candomble practitioners are increasingly being encouraged to establish working relationships with Ifa communities in Nigeria. Recently, Chief Aluko of the Ile Orunmila Temple in Little Haiti, Miami, has founded what amounts to a "mission" church that is gearing up to market a "more correct" Nigerian form of Ifa in the United States (Indigenous Faith of Africa, Inc.).

SCRIPTURES

There are no holy written texts for Orisha worshippers. There are, however, a variety of traditional songs, poems, and stories that are considered to be the source of divine inspiration and worship. Although some collections of these have been published, most worshippers and Awo learn them orally, and they are memorized and recited. The principal divination verses of *obi* and the sixteen major *odus* of Ifa are all committed fully to memory. It is only recently that Nigerian priests have allowed portions of the sixteen odus to be translated from Yoruban and published. The Yoruban language is considered sacred—the voice of the Orishas. As one Awo has described, "When the mouths of the bata drums are opened and the songs of praise are uttered in the sacred Yoruban tongue, the Orishas can be assured that their place in the world of men is secured." Indeed, the processes of learning, remembering, and reciting these oral transmissions is considered to be a religious act, because the worshipper is participating in a lineage of knowledge that has passed down in an unbroken line for countless generations.

The sacred stories tell the histories of the Orishas, their adventures, conflicts, and lessons. Worshippers are to take these stories as personal morality plays and are encouraged to learn from the Orishas' mistakes or to transcend their difficulties as the Orishas once did. For example, one story is about Obatala, the creator of the physical world. According to this story, after creating all things, it came time for Obatala to form humans. Obatala had worked so hard on creation that he decided he needed to relax a bit, so he started to drink. He got drunk, but he still had to finish creating humans. So, he began to make humans, forming each one out of clay. Because he was drunk, his work was careless. As a result, some humans are born deformed or defective in some way. When Obatala was sober again, he was horrified at what he had done. Unfortunately, he could not undo what he had done, and he was punished by Oludumare. There would forever be some imperfection in his world, and he would have to be the mediator of all conflicts. Furthermore, he could never drink again.

The story covers a great deal of ground. It explains why there is human imperfection in the world, and it tells worshippers who have Obatala as their patron how they must act and what they must not do. They cannot drink, and they must learn to take on much responsibility and handle it diplomatically, with what the Yoruba call a "cool head." Obatala's worshippers must become masters of the cool head in order to manifest fully Obatala's ache in the world of humans. They must be responsible so that his responsibility can be fulfilled.

HOLIDAYS, FESTIVALS, RITUALS, AND PRACTICES

There are a variety of fixed and spontaneous rituals and holidays in Orisha tradition. In traditional Yoruban villages, fixed rituals would include a new-year celebration, planting and harvest festivals, and rituals to commemorate special events that define specific communities. Spontaneous festivals and rituals include those conducted to honor individuals fallen in conflict, the reception of good news, or rituals celebrating the healing of an important person. In the Americas, these celebrations are often referred to as *bembes*. Bembes often seem to be held for no other reason than the members of a community want to get out, worship the Orishas, and be seen together. In fact, certain communities have a small bembe every payday.

As in all societies, the Yoruba celebrate births, deaths, marriages, the entrance of children into adulthood, and the initiation of individuals (priests, priestesses, healers) into various branches of their religion. These practices have passed on, in one form or another, into all the Orisha-based faiths found in the Americas. One example is the giving of ileke beads at first initiation. In traditional Ifa societies, this occurs when an individual is a child, but in Western cultures, the ileke ceremony can occur much later in life. The Church of Lukumi Babalu Aye calls the ileke ceremony a baptism. A formal divination is conducted for initiates in order to determine their patron Orisha and their guardian ancestor. Once the patron Orisha is known, corresponding ileke are made and ritually blessed, often with animal and food offerings. Then, they are presented to the initiate to act as a living link between the initiate and his or her Orisha. Initiates are often told to wear the ileke at all times, particularly when they are publicly participating at a bembe. At bembes it is possible to visually determine who worships which Orishas simply by the ileke being worn. Individuals who expect to be mounted by their Orishas may even act the part and show up at bembes wearing the traditional garb of their patrons. When the Orisha possesses or seizes them, they literally become vehicles of the Orishas, with the Orishas acting through them while they remain in trance.

Individual ritual practices are also quite common. Each worshipper is expected to contact or "feed" his Orisha and his guardian ancestor often, sometimes daily. This is done by placing offerings on the Orisha altar or shrine, chanting, and offering prayers. If an Orisha worshipper has a specific request or difficulty, he or she is assigned an Ebbo, a task to perform for the Orisha governing the request. One's patron Orisha is not necessarily responsible for each need or request; over the course of a lifetime, each worshipper will work with all the Orishas at least once. At the beginning of each Ebbo, an offering has to be made to Elegba-Eshu (Eshu), since he is the messenger god of the crossroads, the gatekeeper, and has to be contacted first. Without him, the message will never get through to the Orishas and the Ebbo will not be effective.

After Elegba-Eshu gets his offering, the Ebbo can commence. Often the Ebbo will consist of a simple ritual action (such as

TRANCE POSSESSION

Trance Possession is an example of what religious scholars refer to as an "ecstatic" religious practice. In Orisha-worshipping communities, each individual is ruled by a patron Orisha. At important times, usually during festivals, bembes, or rituals, the Orisha will mount his or her human. This means the nonphysical energy of the Orisha will enter and possess the body of a human in trance. Then the Orishas will use the body of the human to demonstrate its presence and power. Before festivals, individuals will often prepare to be mounted and ridden by dressing up as their Orishas or performing offerings to him or her. Practitioners can ask their Orisha to mount them. Sometimes, however, the possession is unexpected. What this possession looks like to the observer is similar to what occurs in Pentecostal churches when an individual is "taken" by the Holy Spirit. The person will seem to go rigid, will flail about, or dance in time to the drums or music. They may start uttering syllables that are called spirit language. Often such possessed people can perform acts of great strength or endurance that are normally impossible for them. It is not known for sure what the physical causes of trance possession might be, but such ecstasies occur in one form or another in most religions.

candle lighting or a simple offering) that is to be repeated at the same time in the same place over a prescribed number of days or weeks. Sometimes, the worshipper will be asked to perform a more elaborate ritual in sacred places, such as graveyards, railroad tracks, special trees, or street intersections. Occasionally, the Awo or Santero may have to assist the worshipper and perform some kind of additional offering or sacrifice.

CULTURAL EXPRESSIONS

Orisha faiths have deeply influenced many musical forms found in Brazil, the Caribbean, and Cuba. The complex rhythmic structures of bata drumming and the call and response Orisha form of oriki and orin recitation have influenced the development of rumba and salsa music. Such African musical forms have fundamentally shaped several American genres of music as well, ranging from gospel, soul, and jazz to rock-n-roll and hip-hop. The term *cool* is used to describe particularly striking, beautiful, or affecting music in jazz and the blues. This is directly related to the idea of Obatala's ability to keep a cool head, to "chill out" when conflict threatens, and to "keep his cool" when it is important to be diplomatic. All of these turns of phrase have their origins in a uniquely African sensibility of what it means to be a truly powerful leader, one who affects by persuasion, calm intensity, and an invocation of beauty and not by raw power, muscle, or threat.

Just as each Orisha has a color, a number, and items related to it, each also has what is popularly called a *veve*: an elaborate design that is often drawn on the ground in front of an altar or on the bembe grounds where dancing is going to occur. These designs can be drawn with regular chalk or with a compound called *cascarilla*, a chalk that is used specifically for drawing veves or other designs of protection and power in Santeria and Lukumi. The veves are quite beautiful, and elements of the designs are often worked into ceremonial clothing, altar cloths, and other adornments around the home.

FAMILIES AND CHILDREN

In traditional Yoruba society, a child is not named prior to birth. The child is named during a ceremony in which a significant event or circumstance is recalled that occurred immediately before, during, or because of the child's birth. If there is no such event, then objects of symbolic significance, such as a cup of water, a bit of honey, or an honored heirloom, may be presented to the child. If the child reaches for one of the items, this may determine his or her name. The name is intended to reflect the contextual importance of the child and perhaps reveal something of the child's character, because the moment of birth is considered to be of divine circumstance that says something about the person coming into this physical world. After the child is named, there is a ceremony to the Orishas and a feast.

In Orisha communities outside of Yorubaland (Nigeria), the child may be presented with special protecting ileke, and a divination may also be performed along with the naming ceremony and feast. The reading to determine a patron Orisha is generally not performed until the child is older and can understand what is going on. Small children are often considered to be not fully focused in the physical and can be a source of great power and danger to themselves and others. Therefore, they must learn responsibility before they can be fully introduced to the power of the Orishas.

Most of the religious training of children comes from their families and the community at large. Often, an older uncle or aunt (or occasionally a grandparent) will serve as a mentor and take charge of training youngsters in communal respect, ritual, and responsibility. In traditional villages, the entire community helped to raise the children. In Western communities, children are often encouraged to find "godparents," adult individuals who may or may not be related by blood but who are willing to act as guides. Individuals who come to Ifa, Candomble, Santeria, or Lukumi as adults to be initiated, are regarded as symbolic children in the community, and are frequently required to obtain godparents who will assist them in the training necessary to achieve first initiation. In a sense, any convert has to become a member of an extended family.

It is this sense of community that has led some groups of Orisha worshippers to unite their incomes and families together in experimental, planned Yoruban-Ifa villages in the United States. This involves group purchases of land and the establishment of internal political and economic structures that will reproduce some sense of traditional Yoruban village life. One such group, the Kingdom of Oyotunji, is located on private land outside of Sheldon, South Carolina. The kingdom grew out of the vision of Oseijeman Adefunmi, one of the first Africans to be fully invested in Ifa priesthoods in Africa and in Cuba (the West). He founded the African Theological Archministry, Inc., in 1959. In 1970, the African Theological Archministry, Inc., established the village in South Carolina in order to provide a safe environment for people interested in studying and preserving African cultural traditions from Yorubaland. Each year, the village kingdom hosts a series of festivals that are open to the public. In accordance with traditional practice, the Kingdom of Oyotunji conducts a yearly divination in order to determine what can be expected in the coming year. A divination for the world is conducted, and divinations for African Americans and the United States are also rendered. All these readings are available on the community Website: http://www.oyotunjivillage.net/oyo2_001.htm.

CONTROVERSIES

There is probably no Ifa practice that causes more controversy, at least in the United States, than the periodic practice of animal sacrifice. The attitude toward animal sacrifice in the United States is often influenced by Hollywood misunderstandings about the purpose and frequency of the practice. What many Americans choose to forget is that most ancient cultures, including that of the ancient Israelites, practiced some form of animal sacrifice (the words "sacred" and "sacrifice" have the same root). In all Ifa and Vodu faiths, animal sacrifice is the first part of a ritual that involves a ceremonial meal. The animal is always consumed by the community; therefore, the sacrificial element is ritualized slaughter. These practices are similar to those rituals practiced by Jews and Muslims to ensure that meat is kosher or *hallal*. As in ancient Israelite practices, the blood of an animal is considered sacred as it contains the life or soul of the animal. Because the Orishas are being asked to perform a special function, they must be fed or be asked to join in a ritual feast. The blood of the sacrificed animal is their portion of the feast. Animals that are to be sacrificed are frequently raised solely for that purpose and are treated very well because they are considered vehicles of worship. The killing is done quickly and is considered more humane than the techniques used in most slaughterhouses today. Animals are generally sacrificed only for special requests or initiations. Worshippers who feed their Orishas daily commonly use plant products, candles, or alcohol as offerings.

Despite its religious significance in Orisha worship, animal sacrifice has led to controversy and legal questions. In 1993, the U.S. Supreme Court rendered a very important decision. It overturned the ruling of the city of Hialeah, Florida, to prevent the Church of Lukumi Babalu Aye from performing its religious duties by specifically prohibiting the practice of animal sacrifice. A group of citizens in Hialeah had convinced the city government to ban animal sacrifice under the pretense that it was cruel and primitive. As animal sacrifice is required to complete certain ceremonies and initiations, the church felt it could not function as a community without the practice. A state court upheld the city's decision, forcing the church to take the case to the Supreme Court. The church was able to demonstrate with a great deal of evidence that the city of Hialeah was simply afraid of this practice and had singled it out while at the same time specifically exempting similar practices of kosher slaughter. The Supreme Court ruled that the city of Hialeah had violated the First and Fourteenth amendments of the U.S. Constitution and had shown quite a bit of ignorance, intolerance, and bigotry in doing so. The case set a precedent, and in several U.S. cities (Chicago, New York, Los Angeles, and Atlanta), laws now exist that specifically allow for and help to regulate the practice of animal sacrifice within city limits. Most of these laws even address how sacrificial animals are to be housed.

The practice of animal sacrifice has also begun to divide members of the larger Orisha worshipping community. As more Westerners are brought into Orisha worshipping faiths, some have decided to forego the practice of animal sacrifice, claiming it is no longer needed and is inappropriate for practitioners in the West. The Ifa organization begun by Philip Niemark, for example, argues that the shedding of blood is no longer necessary, because the Orishas can be (and usually are) effectively fed with plant and alcohol products. More traditionally oriented Ifa organizations and leaders have accused Neimark of a kind of latent racism, saying that as a white practitioner, he is having difficulty with black African practices. From Neimark's perspective, his argument is similar to that made by Jewish rabbis in the second century after the Jewish Temple in Jerusalem was destroyed and proper animal sacrifice became impossible. Rabbinical authorities argued that God could be satisfied with the offering of prayer, because God does not actually need the blood of an animal. In truth, the practice is a convincing prop that says more about human dedication than the desire and nature of the Divine. In any case, the issue will probably not go away but will be become a litmus test of what will be considered traditional, orthodox Orisha worship against more liberal interpretations. This is an example of a division that commonly occurs when a religious tradition is in the process of becoming a more generally universalized faith.

IN THE WORLD TODAY

Orisha-based faiths have many millions of adherents. Ironically, recent events in the nation of Nigeria have pushed native

Yoruban Ifa believers to reach out to Candomble and Santeria-Lukumi practitioners in the Americas, where their traditions can be preserved. Nigeria is a developing country that is undergoing many tumultuous changes because of its rich oil reserves and diverse religious population. Nigerian oil fields are being developed by Western multinational corporations, which often do not take into consideration local environments or traditional native populations. Religious conflicts frequently erupt between the Muslim majority, a powerful Christian minority, and a score of African traditional belief systems. The latter, mostly concerned with trying to preserve native religions and cultures in the face of the multiple threats presented by the challenges of increased religious persecution and money, often end up on the losing side of these battles. Institutions such as the Church of Lukumi Babalu Aye have been established in the West in an attempt to help direct the development and preservation of Orisha worship.

Orisha worship is not, as some might believe, only for Africans or those with African ancestry. The religion is quite colorblind. Many of the most important individuals working in traditional Ifa, such as the popular writer Awo Fa'Lokun Fatumbi, are, in fact, of Anglo origin. As Fatumbi explains, all humans originated in Africa, therefore, all humans are actually African. A Babalawo working in Kansas City, Missouri, elaborated on this concept: "The Orisha are universal forces that Africans have visualized as black because most Africans are black, in the same way that most Europeans visualized Jesus as white because they were white, when Jesus was probably not white at all." At the same time, this commentator felt that it might be important for whites in the United States who come to Ifa to experience divinity the way blacks do, because doing so might help them to get beyond what is familiar to them so that they can see divinity in all things. In a world that has been so divided by race and is now experiencing the effects of ignoring the natural world, the commentator believes that experiencing the power of the Orishas and the ancestors might help to correct the imbalances created by hatred, fear, and ignorance. "We must bring divinity into the world," he said. "When you allow yourself to be 'taken' by the Orishas, when you acknowledge the force of the Orishas, of nature, in your life, then you understand your place, you can work for your peace and the peace of others."

7

Falun Gong
(Falun Dafa)

The path for cultivating gong lies in one's heart.

—Li Hongzhi, "Cultivation of Xinxing," Falun Gong

INTRODUCTION

Western audiences first became aware of the *Falun Gong* movement after the Chinese Communist government began a series of highly publicized crackdowns against practitioners after a ten-thousand-person Falun Gong demonstration for freedom of practice was staged in Beijing on April 25, 1999. The Chinese government exerted considerable energy in encouraging Western media not to make too much of the persecutions nor to take the claims of Falun Gong practitioners too seriously. This, of course, only made some in the West more interested in discovering what the government in Beijing was trying to hide. The Chinese government made the same claim about Falun Gong that is often made by the Western media when describing a vilified or deviant religious faith group. Government authorities claimed that Falun Gong followers were brainwashed and were forced to follow a deranged leader. They contended that the practices were dangerous and led to psychotic behavior and that Falun Gong was *xiejiao*—a crooked teaching—a pejorative term much like the word cult in the United States or sect in Europe.

Chinese governments have periodically persecuted religious groups, particularly Pentecostal Christians, Muslims, Tibetan Buddhists, or groups that may be political with some religious trappings. Among those targeted groups were the White Lotus movement of the nineteenth century and the Boxer Rebellion of the early twentieth century. Such persecution has occurred throughout recent Chinese history and is not solely a practice of the Communist Party. Something about Falun Gong, however, was different. The leadership and regular lay practitioners resisted the government in a way that was quite unusual. First, there was the large demonstration of at least ten thousand people, staged in front of the residential area of the Communist Party in Beijing. As arrests began, practitioners of Falun Gong began to show up in large numbers whenever foreign state dignitaries were due to arrive in Beijing. They protested in front of foreign diplomats, a move that was specifically designed to shame the Chinese government and to make the authorities lose face, because social control had been lost. Some practitioners immolated themselves (committed suicide by setting themselves on fire) in public to protest government harassment. Following such tactics, the Chinese government adopted a policy of "anything goes" to deal with Falun Gong practitioners. Police seized people in their homes. Some individuals were incarcerated in mental institutions; hunger strikers were forcibly fed.

Followers of Falun Gong have appealed directly to Western nationals, describing their plight in terms that have strong symbolic importance in the Western media: holocaust, genocide, civil disobedience, and torture. They maintain that their spirituality consists of traditional Chinese practices that have resulted in greater health and well-being for the vast majority of their membership. They argue that people come to Falun Gong because of its effectiveness. In fact, many Gong practitioners, including the founder, Li Hongzhi, maintain that Falun Gong is not actually a religion at all but a combination of new and old sciences. Their literature claims that between 955 and 1,000 people have been "persecuted to death" in China, a number that Western observers have indicated is impossible to verify but well within the "bounds of possibility." The Chinese government continues to denounce Falun Gong as a dangerous, mind-warping, society-destroying doctrine that causes people to abandon their families and go insane.[9]

Most scholars believe that both sides have exaggerated Falun Gong membership numbers. They contend that the Chinese government wants to downplay what it considers an "incident" while it continues to maintain that the movement is large enough to be dangerous. On the other hand, Falun Gong leadership wants to demonstrate that the movement is vital and growing because of its effectiveness and in spite of government persecution. In the midst of these two warring propaganda campaigns, several facts concerning this movement have emerged:

- Falun Gong is a unique spiritual-religious movement that is definitely rooted in the ongoing interaction between traditional modes of Chinese spiritual practice and a modernizing Chinese society.

- The Chinese government does have some legitimate reasons to fear Falun Gong (though not necessarily from a Western standpoint)—not as a practice within itself but because of what the existence of the organization and its specific methods suggest about changes in Chinese society.

- Contrary to what it claims, Falun Gong is more than simply a recapitulation of ancient Taoist and Buddhist meditation exercises. Although these are at the core of the practice, there are many things that Falun Gong has in common with other religious movements and Taoist schools in China. The movement also contains cosmological elements and moral and ethical teachings that are unique to it, which dedicated practitioners are encouraged to adopt in order to further their cultivation. Such unique differences do not mean these teachings are dangerous; in fact, these cosmological and ethical teachings are not what triggered the hostile response of the Chinese government.

FOUNDATIONS

Li Hongzhi, the founder of *Falun Dafa* (the original name of the Falun Gong movement), introduced his teachings in 1992 through the Qigong Research Association of China, which was a loose consortium of *qigong* schools that were considered perfectly legitimate at the time. Li Hongzhi later withdrew his movement from the association because the purposes of the association and those of Falun Dafa did not coincide. Falun Dafa began to grow rapidly, and Chinese officials became concerned that even Communist party members were joining the movement. The Chinese government refused to allow the group to join any other associations, and members were left without any legal authorization or protection. Li Hongzhi relocated to New York State in 1996, but he keeps in touch with his worldwide following through the Internet and via the annual Falun Dafa/Gong Experience Sharing Conference. The group was declared illegal by the Chinese government in July 1999.

Various *gong* or personal cultivation techniques involving meditation or simple physical movements (such as tai chi) have a long history in Chinese culture and have been especially popular since the 1970s. Many spiritual teachers in China have made unique claims about their interpretations and applications of these practices, so in this sense, Falun Gong is not unique. In a nutshell, gong is a form of Chinese self-help that is designed to increase feelings of well-being, improve health, and foster self-awareness and moral behavior. Traditional Taoist, Buddhist, and Confucian schools in China have all taught similar techniques of gong. Li Hongzhi claims that his teaching of Falun Gong (the exercise practices) or Falun Dafa (the meditation, philosophical, and ethical components) constitutes the most complete system of self-cultivation that has yet been compiled, combining Taoist, Buddhist, and Confucian principles. Central to the moral practice of Falun Gong is Li's emphasis on five physical exercises. These exercises and their underlying principles strengthen an individual's *shinshing* or "heart-moral nature." An individual with strong shinshing is more resistant to disease and leads a longer, more successful life. Additionally, strong shinshing can make a person impervious to the influence of evil forces, such as demons that might influence poor behavior.

According to Qigong principles, located in the lower abdomen or *dan-tien* of each person is a spinning wheel of energy. This wheel is said to be the "seat of power." Li refers to this cluster of energy as the *falun* or *law wheel* and teaches that this internal wheel is each person's personal representation of the Wheel of Dharma that is common to Buddhist thought.

Falun Gong literature represents this law wheel as a spinning swastika around which four smaller swastikas and four small yin-yang symbols revolve.[10]

According to Li, practitioners of Falun Gong participate in a method that allows each person to turn this personal wheel of dharma. This Falun, once attuned to Li's teaching through the practice, is a live, self-aware energy substance that absorbs positive energy from the universe and neutralizes negative energy trapped in the body. The Falun is said to rotate at the same rate as the universe; in cultivating the practice, an individual begins to become one with the cosmos. Li has commented that the Falun he "implants" into practitioners through the practice spins constantly and never has to be renewed or restarted once it is put in place. Receiving Li's Falun through his teachings puts an individual under the protection of Li's dharma bodies. Perfected cultivation and protection from evil is inevitable if the disciple follows the teachings with sincerity and to the letter. In this way, a dedicated practitioner can perfect his or her cultivation and move up through higher and higher levels of existence.

Li Hongzhi has also publicly stated that Falun Gong will protect an individual from interference by an expanding group of aliens (extraterrestrial beings) that he believes have gradually been infiltrating human society since the beginning of the twentieth century. According to Li, these aliens are responsible for most of the great technological advances that have been made, particularly in the computer and biogenetic sciences (especially cloning). He claims that the long-term goal of the aliens is to form genetic links with humans through a cloning process that will enable them to gradually take over and conquer human society. According to Li, Falun Gong will enable practitioners to thwart these biological attempts at human colonization by aliens.

Li Hongzhi and Falun Gong practitioners have repeatedly stated that their doctrines and practices do not constitute a religion but are to be understood as a type of science with techniques that can be tested and demonstrated. He has also claimed that Falun Gong does not contradict any other religious practice or preclude any other faith claim.

SCRIPTURES

Li Hongzhi has written two books, *Zhuan Falun* (*Revolving the Law Wheel*) and *China Falun Gong*, which outline the basics of Falun Gong and Falun Dafa for disciples. In theory, no one is compelled to read them. Practitioners are encouraged to familiarize themselves with the texts, but they do not necessarily operate as scripture. The books contain summaries of the principles and exercises of Falun Gong, as well as moral and ethical precepts that are recommended as appropriate for individuals practicing the gong.

Practitioners are encouraged to train with local groups, and afterwards they are to attend a free, nine-day seminar, where they learn to integrate the principles of Falun Dafa into their lives. This international seminar, called the Experience Sharing Conference, is held once a year. All Falun Gong practitioners can attend. According to Li Hongzhi, practitioners can take as long as they like to learn the principles and exercises of Falun Gong. They can come and go as they please; there are no fees, dues, or mandatory attendance requirements.

Li's books advise students which sexual practices, mental activities, and emotional states he considers appropriate and inappropriate for cultivating shinshing. It is in this sense that his work is more than simply a set of physical exercises. He presents himself as an authority who can mandate absolutes in moral and ethical behavior. He asserts that bad actions generate a black substance called *karma*, which is a kind of "soul sludge" that ends up tainting a person's mental, spiritual, and physical organism. The practice of appropriate behavior and the five exercises of the gong transform this black substance into a white substance, which signifies the purification of the body. As this white substance develops, a *third eye* (located on the forehead between the existing eyes) opens up and enables a more perfect clarity of vision and calm that allows a practitioner to teach and heal others.

In Li Hongzhi's appendices to *Zhuan Falun*, much emphasis is placed on following the teachings of Master Li exactly and to the letter. Falun Dafa practitioners and trainers are warned against following any other kind of Qigong training: "Dafa disciples are forbidden to mix their practice with the practices of any other cultivation way (those who go awry are always these kinds of people). Whoever ignores this warning is himself responsible for any problems that might occur."[11] Trainers are discouraged from using their own experiences of the practice or to interpret Li's teaching in any distinctly personal way. Such practices may seem very strange or suspicious to a Western audience but probably reflect traditional Chinese teaching strategies.

WORLDVIEW AND ORGANIZATION

Despite Li's sense that the world may be in crisis because of the ongoing alien invasion, Falun Gong does not promote any *millenarian* beliefs. Li allows himself to be called a "living Buddha" and a "Taoist master," but such titles are common for leaders of Eastern religious movements. Li does not encourage anyone to worship him, but as the teacher of the movement, he is given great respect and some reverence. Fundraising or other kinds of monetary gain in the name of Falun Gong is not allowed. Individuals who want to become trainers and open practice facilities have to raise their own money to do so. They are to receive no fee or compensation for their own private benefit. It is on this basis that Falun Gong practitioners can make the claim that their movement is completely free and voluntary and that they have no leaders or disciples but only practitioners who are all equally committed to personal development. Membership lists are not kept, attendance is free and voluntary, and it is therefore quite difficult to determine how many Falun Gong members there are in China and elsewhere.

There are some indications that the movement may be a bit more organized than Li claims. Only one academic work has studied the movement: *The Mystery of China's Falun Gong: Its Rise and Sociological Implications* (written by John Wong and William T. Liu). The book indicates that immediately prior to the 1999 crackdown, the Falun Gong movement was able to report that the Chinese branch of the organization had "39 teaching centers, 1,900 instruction centers, and 28,000 practice sites."[12] This suggests a large, mobilized membership with extensive communication between groups.

Some scholars have speculated that the vigorous use of the Internet by Falun Gong practitioners has been the key to the movement's growth and success. Indeed, since Li's departure from China, Falun Gong practitioners have relied heavily on the Internet to keep in contact with their cultivation master and each other. The Internet has also been used to spread news about Falun Gong to a world audience and to encourage the world to put pressure on the Chinese government to stop ongoing persecution. Thus, despite Li's apparent suspicion that the computer may be alien technology, his group certainly finds it useful.

There is little evidence that most Falun Gong practitioners are aware of or pay much attention to the more unusual aspects of Li's cosmology. It is not even clear how much the rank and file membership even reads his texts. Most Falun Gong practitioners are sold on their experiences of increased peace of mind and health resulting from their cultivation practices. Recently, a number of Falun Gong practitioners demonstrated their exercises on the Mall in Washington, D.C. An informal interview indicated that out of a group of twenty or so, only two had actually heard of Li's special concerns about aliens, and only about half had read any portion of his texts. A few expressed some surprise about Li's views, but no one seemed very concerned about them. These responses seem to confirm that Li has never suggested that Falun Gong practitioners take his cosmological teachings on the same faith that they are to take his exercises.

RITUALS, PRACTICES, AND HOLIDAYS

There are no official holidays or rituals in the practice of Falun Gong. The birthday of the founder is not commemorated, nor are there any seasonal celebrations specific to the religion. This is consistent with the movement's claim that it is not really a religion. The only regular ritual features are the five daily exercises. These exercises are traditional Qigong positions combined with meditation and visualization practices that are not essentially different from practices found in other Qigong schools. The exercises have typical Qigong names such as "Buddha Showing a Thousand Hands," a possible reference to the bodhisattva, Avalokitesvara, or Kuan Yin[13] and are similar to postures and movements found in other Taoist Qigong schools. Three of the exercises are standing practices that involve highly stylized movements of the arms. Two of the exercises involve sitting for rather lengthy periods while performing other arm or hand movements. There are variations in the movements depending on whether the practitioner is male or female. Li claims that his movements are particularly powerful and effective even though they are considered relatively simple to learn.

In traditional Taoist practice, it is not uncommon for masters to develop their own unique approaches to ancient practices or even to attribute special powers to their personal teachings. In many Qigong schools, trained practitioners, once proficient in the arts they are mastering, are expected to go off on their own and further develop their teacher's approach. Li Hongzhi insists that his method be followed to the letter. In this regard, Falun Dafa most resembles the Scientology movement in the West, whose practitioners and teachers have to follow the stated methods of the teacher exactly. (Like Falun Gong, Scientology claims to be both a science and a religion.)

CONTROVERSIES

Certain aspects of Li's teaching might be considered controversial by some Western observers, particularly statements that he has made against gays and interracial relationships, and his insinuations that there are different heavens for different racial groups. Some Westerners might also look askance at the claim that he is an incarnate Buddha or at his concerns about alien invasion. These views and attitudes, however, are not the main concern of the Chinese government.

Scholars have advanced many possible reasons for the systematic persecution of Falun Gong supporters in China. Historically, most Chinese governments have been suspicious of any large-scale political or religious movement that may encourage individual citizens to be more loyal to it than to the state. Such concerns have prompted Chinese states for at least a millennium to persecute Buddhists, Christians, Taoists, and Muslims along with many smaller religious movements from time to time. Professor Michael Lestz has argued that Chinese governments have generally reacted quite vigorously to "perceived political/religious threats or antagonisms," [14] so that the current government response in Beijing is more in keeping with Chinese historical habit than with Communism particularly. Such movements are commonly believed to herald the end of an empire and are often quite vigorously suppressed. This would especially be the case if—as Falun Gong leaders and some observers have claimed—the number of Falun Gong disciples far outnumbered the membership of the Communist Party in China.

Other scholars have noted that the international nature of Falun Gong may be of considerable concern to the government. The Communist party has attempted to place a variety of state-run controls on Internet and computer services in the country, but the nature of the technologies simply outstrips their efforts. Falun Gong is a movement that has gained much of its momentum by using the Internet effectively and, from a governmental perspective, that connection puts the movement beyond its control. The government's concerns, specifically, are that the Falun Gong movement will gain international support, that Internet use may increase uncontrolled Western access to China's peoples, and that it might further be utilized to apply pressure by Western interests in China in unpredictable ways. China has repeatedly demanded Li Hongzhi's extradition, claiming that he is responsible for the deaths of many people who practice his techniques. He is also charged with organizing demonstrations without permits. In hundreds of cases, Chinese authorities have harassed and arrested Falun Gong practitioners in violation of the United Nations Universal Declaration of Humans Rights, which China has signed. The response of the U.S. Congress to repressive Chinese actions against the Falun Gong has taken the form of two resolutions unanimously passed in November 1999, which strongly criticize the Chinese crackdown. The United States has coupled these resolutions with a continued refusal to turn Li Hongzhi over to Chinese authorities.

One final factor influencing the Chinese government's actions may be related to how Falun Gong practitioners responded to initial government persecutions. Prior to the April 1999 demonstration, Falun Gong was one of several movements that the government had moved against to reestablish a certain level of predictability and order. Some years earlier, China had enacted a religious freedom policy, which allowed for a greater degree of religious toleration as long as religious movements registered and followed certain general guidelines. From 1996 through 1998, however, the government launched a program of general persecution against many different groups.

It was soon after this that the large and unexpected Falun Gong demonstration occurred. The demonstrators provocatively positioned themselves right in front of the Communist Party residential quarters at *Tiananmen Square*, the site of pro-democracy demonstrations of the early 1990s. Even sympathetic observers admitted that such a performance seemed to be designed for maximum impact and reaction. In the wake of the extremely aggressive persecutions that followed and have continued in China, Falun Gong followers have continued their own rather aggressive resistance to authority.

Chinese officials have been quite alarmed at the large number of people Falun Gong leaders have been able to mobilize for their demonstrations. For them, such large-scale demonstrations are proof of a rampant subversive force that could undermine social order.

In the United States, advertising the plight of Falun Gong practitioners in China has become one of the major proselytizing devices of the international movement. For lay observers in the United States, the continued emphasis on the persecution of Falun Gong practitioners in China often causes some confusion.

Scholars posit that the persecution simply reflects the Chinese government's fear that the group has the power to turn people into disloyal citizens and that Chinese officials fear the loss of control and loss of face or national pride if this occurs. Such reasons are not sufficient for ordinary Americans to justify persecution, and most Americans do not believe that any religious group should be singled out and persecuted simply because of its beliefs. Nevertheless, many Americans harbor a vague suspicion that there must be some reason the Chinese government is "going after" Falun Gong practitioners.

IN THE WORLD TODAY

John Wong and William Liu have noted that in China, at least prior to the crackdown, Falun Gong membership was highest among older members of society, individuals for whom many of the new economic and social reforms were not working. For Wong and Liu, this suggested that the Chinese government may have some additional concerns about the growing population of elderly people. China has a population of over 1 billion citizens. The possibility of many individuals who may not consider the state to be adequate for their care and who instead give their loyalty to a man living overseas in a rich Western country could definitely cause concern for Chinese authorities. The persecutions continue, although there is some evidence that they have recently become more infrequent. The

Chinese government says it now has the movement under control. Falun Gong representatives disagree. Wong and Liu have argued that the influence of Falun Gong in China will probably decline in the short term but that its global membership may continue to grow. Total membership numbers are unknown, but Falun Gong Websites claim many millions of practitioners.

8

Neo-Paganism and Wicca

And you who seek to know Me,
know that your seeking and yearning will avail you not,
unless you know the Mystery:
for if that which you seek,
you find not within yourself,
you will never find it without.
For behold, I have been with you from the beginning,
and I am that which is attained at the end of desire.

—Attributed to Doreen Valiente,
Charge of the Goddess

INTRODUCTION

Of all the New Religious Movements described in this volume, Neo-Paganism and Wicca are perhaps the most difficult to define. The refusal of many Neo-Pagans and Wiccans to completely classify themselves in organizational or doctrinal terms contributes to this situation. This has not kept Neo-Paganism or Wicca from growing. In fact, forms of Neo-Paganism and Wicca are often counted among those New Religious Movements that are growing the most rapidly in the United States. Although absolute numbers are impossible to determine, because of organizational inconsistency and the tendency of Neo-Pagans and Wiccans to be solitary spiritual seekers, it is believed that they number in the hundreds of thousands.

The simplest definition of Neo-Paganism/Wicca is that it is a form of organized nature worship. Neo-Pagans and Wiccans are informed and inspired by mythological stories and ritual practices that are drawn primarily from pre-Christian European and Mediterranean sources. Adding to the confusion is that all Wiccans are Neo-Pagans but not all Neo-Pagans are Wiccans. Wiccans tend to focus on rituals and mythologies derived from Celtic, Norman, and Anglo-Saxon sources. Neo-Pagans derive their principal inspiration from premonotheistic Middle Eastern, Egyptian, Greek, or Roman sources. Neo-Pagans who focus on German-Scandinavian mythologies often refer to themselves as being of "The Troth," "Asatru," or "Odinists." Some seek to rediscover the practices of the ancient Druids; still others attempt to resurrect pre-Christian Russian, Gypsy, Romanian, or Finnish beliefs and practices. Native American, African, and Asian sources are also influential. Both Neo-Pagans and Wiccans are interested in renewing and reconstructing forms of ancient worship and ritual that focus on the divinity found in nature and natural forces.

Neo-Pagans and Wiccans may or may not use the words "witch" or "witchcraft," to describe who they are or what they do. Neo-Pagans and Wiccans, whether or not they use the word "witch," seek to rediscover old patterns of belief and practice

ABOUT WITCHES, WITCHCRAFT, AND SATANISM

Wiccans often explain that Wicca comes from a Celtic/Anglo-Saxon term *wiccae*, which means "craft of the wise." In fact, it is the term *witch* (from Anglo Saxon *witta*, meaning a clever or wise individual) that carries this meaning. The term *wiccae* means "to bend or alter" and refers to an ability to change reality according to the will of the Divine. The Website www.religioustolerance.org indicates that there are seventeen different ways in which the terms *witchcraft* and *witch* can be used in American culture. Wiccans use these terms very specifically to mean someone (witch) who practices the rituals and techniques (witchcraft) of Wicca.

Satanism is an entirely different New Religious Movement. It has its own churches and organizations and is distinct from Neo-Paganism/Wicca in a number of ways. Satanists often assume the same kind of dualist (God vs. Satan) worldview as many Christians do; they simply worship the "bad guy" rather than a good God. Alternately, many Satanists are in fact quite agnostic and see Satan as a metaphor for natural human desires and impulses that are unnaturally suppressed by standard religious practice. Neo-Pagans/Wiccans do not believe in the Christian form of dualism. Since they do not believe in Satan, they cannot be said to worship him.

Although Satanists may use some of the same symbols as Neo-Pagans, such as the pentagram, or five-pointed star, the meanings that are assigned to these symbols are quite different. For Neo-Pagans/Wiccans, for example, the pentagram represents the four natural elements: earth, air, fire, and water plus spirit. For Satanists, the pentagram often represents a stylized human form expressing its will on the cosmos. This is an important distinction. Neo-Pagans/Wiccans desire to come into harmony or unity with nature. Satanists often speak of desiring to work their will on nature and the human world. Ironically, some Satanists often see Neo-Pagans/Wiccans as being not substantially different from the Christians around them. Finally, Satanists may or may not be nature worshippers; Neo-Pagans/Wiccans, almost without exception, are.

that can link them to nature, to the seasons, to animals, and to other humans in organic, life-affirming ways. Neo-Pagans and Wiccans see themselves as restorers of a human spirituality that existed before the time of dogmas, churches, creeds, divine punishment, and religious warfare. Most are not anti-Christian as is sometimes claimed. Instead, they attempt to show where and how Christians borrowed from the very pagans they often sought to convert. In fact, Neo-Pagans and Wiccans borrow from Christianity or any other religion when they find something that strikes their fancy, is seen as helpful, or is in accordance with their personal beliefs and practices.

FOUNDATIONS

Neo-Pagans and Wiccans claim that their beliefs and practices spring from ancient sources. There are, however, three main historical influences from which the modern Neo-Pagan movement developed, and these date back to the nineteenth century. The first influence is linked to an ongoing occult revival. The second influence is an artistic and literary style often called Romanticism. Romantic authors or artists often express the alienating effects of the industrial revolution and nostalgically seek to return to a simpler time. The third influence comes from the development of anthropology and archaeology, disciplines that first introduced earlier cultures to Western public scrutiny.

These three influences were melded together by an individual who first taught what would become known as Wicca in Britain during the 1920s. His name was Gerald Gardner. As some scholars have put it, "It is possible that modern paganism could have emerged without Gerald Gardner, but without his influence it would have been quite a different phenomenon."[15] Gardner made the claim that he had been initiated into "the Old Religion" by an elderly woman whom the locals referred to as Old Dorothy. Gardner created a simple set of rituals and promoted the view that pre-Christian Celtic worship focused on the image of a Great Goddess. It was time for this religion to reemerge from a largely forgotten past and for the followers of the goddess to reawaken her energy and spirit. He called the religion "Wicca" (from Anglo-Saxon, meaning "to bend or alter"), and he referred to its practitioners as witches.

Alex Sanders, who first labored to be initiated into a Gardnerian *coven*, went on to develop his own interpretation of Wicca. He taught his system to Janet and Stewart Farrar who developed Wicca still further. The three types of Wicca—Gardnerian, Alexanderian, and Farrarian—are often collectively termed *British Tradition Wicca* or *Brid-Trad*. All three schools maintain some of the distinctively Wiccan elements of Neo-Pagan practice. From the 1950s to the 1960s, Brid-Trad began to make its way into American culture, largely through the efforts of American witches Ray Buckland and Gavin and Yvonne Frost. By the 1970s, American Wicca had become a unique entity unto itself, often allying with political groups and movements and spawning many significant subgroups of Wicca. These forms of Wicca, along with the other kinds of Neo-Paganism that began to emerge at the same time, generated a greater Neo-Pagan community that is extremely complex and diverse. Today, there are substantial Neo-Pagan/Wiccan communities across North America, in every European country, Australia, South Africa, and Japan.

SCRIPTURES

There are no authorized Neo-Pagan/Wiccan scriptures. Instead, Neo-Pagan/Wiccans are noted for wide-ranging reading habits. Many are amateur researchers, and most pride themselves on being voracious readers. Conversations with groups of Neo-Pagans often revolve around the latest volumes that have been added to their libraries. Neo-Pagans/Wiccans enjoy reading compilations of Greek, Roman, Celtic, or Germanic mythology and folklore as well as texts that link spirituality with science or technology. Many Neo-Pagans, particularly those affiliated with the Church of All Worlds, glean metaphysical-spiritual insights from science fiction-fantasy literature, especially the works of Robert Heinlein, Ursula Le Guin, and Marian Zimmer Bradley.

Neo-Pagans/Wiccans are expected to educate themselves about the possibilities of being pagan. This is even true for those who join a particular community and are assigned texts to read by their instructor-initiators. This process of education and instruction is often written down in a personal diary or record that is called a *Book of Shadows* or *Grimoire*. Thus, each individual has an accounting of what worked for him or her personally and can then share with others.

There are several Neo-Pagan/Wiccan authors whose writings, at least in North American communities, have achieved what can loosely be called canonical status: Margo Adler, Starhawk, Scott Cunningham, Ray Buckland, Ted Andrews, Doreen Valiente, Janet and Stewart Farrar, Amber K, Silver Ravenwolf, Diane Stein, D.J. Conway, Gerald Gardner, and Merlin Stone. Texts that approach this canonical status include: *Drawing Down the Moon, The Spiral Dance, Wicca: A Guide for the Solitary Practitioner, Book of Witchcraft, Positive Magic, True Magick, The Witches Bible* (Farrar), *ABC's of Witchcraft, The Chalice and the Blade,* and *When God Was a Woman.*

WORLDVIEW AND ORGANIZATION

There is no one universal worldview that all Neo-Pagans/Wiccans hold. One online information source indicates that depending on how the term *God* is defined, Neo-Pagans might be classified as monotheists, duotheists (two gods), polytheists, pantheists, or atheists. Depending on circumstances or audience, a single Neo-Pagan could adopt any one of these postures to make a point. A popular saying in the American Neo-Pagan community claims that if you put three pagans in a room together to discuss one topic, you might get up to five (or six) opinions, because at least two will change their minds, and at least one has probably never made up his mind to begin with. It is more accurate to say that Neo-Pagans have a fluid understanding of divinity. While most might agree that all of creation-nature probably emerges from a single source, it manifests itself in a multiplicity of forms. The aspect of nature that one concentrates on then manifests itself in a concept of divinity. If one focuses on the underlying unity of things, one thinks in monotheistic terms. If one focuses on the complementary nature of seeming opposites (good/bad, hot/cold, dark/light, male/female), there is a tendency toward a duotheistic view and so on.

That being said, there are some general principles that most pagans share—a kind of generic Neo-Paganism/Wicca:

- Most Neo-Pagans/Wiccans emphasize the female principle of divinity, although many will also seek to balance female and male expressions of the divine. Most Neo-Pagans will say that the stress on the female side is an attempt to compensate for the millennia of mainstream religious emphasis on male images of divinity—and that they are trying to address this imbalance. Closely linked to this is the reverence with which Neo-Pagans/Wiccans regard the planet Earth as an embodiment of divinity.

- Most Neo-Pagans/Wiccans maintain that there is a law of return in the universe: What one sows, so one will reap. In other words, what goes around comes around. Wicca has codified this concept into two principles: "The Wiccan Rede," which in its short form means as long as your actions are not harming or impeding another, you are free to do anything. The second principle is the Law of Three-Fold Return: Whatever you do, good or ill, it will rebound on you threefold or three times over. These principles state what most Neo-Pagans/Wiccans assume—that there is a general universal law of justice and balance inherent in the order of things that will reward one appropriately in this life or the next.

- Most (although not all) Neo-Pagans/Wiccans believe in and practice what might be called magic. Magic, in accordance with the principles just described, is generally to be used for constructive, protective, and generative purposes. The literature suggests that one should learn balance and control before attempting any form of magic. Many Neo-Pagan/Wiccan magical practices actually resemble ritualized prayer, and most are used for healing, petitions, blessings, and the regular things that one might pray for.

Neo-Pagans often cultivate a robust sense of humor about their beliefs and practices, stressing (as the Wiccan Charge of the Goddess states) the importance of "reverence and mirth" in their religion. Some go even a step further and focus on "discordian" behavior, a difficult to define attitude that may emerge if rituals are determined to be too serious. Discordian behavior may erupt as a series of bad puns, jokes, and plain silliness in the middle of the most serious ritual moments. For pagans, such antics serve as humbling reminders of the principle of divine chaos.

Just as there is no fixed worldview, there is no single Neo-Pagan/Wiccan organizational structure. Most Neo-Pagans/Wiccans in the United States are solitary practitioners and are not formally aligned with any particular Neo-Pagan/Wiccan organization. Many Neo-Pagans/Wiccans discover their religious affiliation through publications or association. Neo-Pagans/Wiccans do not proselytize. A common perception of those who have embraced Neo-Paganism is, "It [the religion] found me, I did not find it."

A simple description of just two Neo-Pagan/Wiccan organizations demonstrates the wide diversity in the American community. The first Wiccan Church to be incorporated was founded in 1968 by Gavin and Yvonne Frost. The Frosts, who were pioneers in Wicca organization and publishing in the United States, took up where Alexanderian Wicca left off. They founded the Church and School of Wicca in order to disseminate their interpretation of Wicca to an American audience and were among the first Wiccans to confront state and federal authorities in order to do so. They spearheaded the efforts to make Wicca-Witchcraft a recognized religion in 1972 and reaffirmed that status before a federal appeals court in 1985.

In addition to writing and publishing numerous books about Wicca, the Frosts were instrumental in starting Wiccan chaplaincy programs in the prison system, and they began one of the first organized, comprehensive Wicca correspondence

WICCAN CHARGE OF THE GODDESS

This poem (in its many variations) has become a classic of Wiccan ritual and is used at every Esbat (full and new moon). It is said to have been written by Doreen Valiente, a woman who influenced the British Tradition and the Farrars.

Listen to the words of the Great Mother: she who was of old also called among wo/man by many names: Artemis, Astarte, Athene, Dione, Astorah, Inanna, Melusine, Aphrodite, Cerridwen, Diana, Arianrhod, Isis, Bride . . .

Whenever ye have need of anything, once in the month, and better it be when the moon is full, then shall ye assemble in some secret place, and adore the spirit of me, who am Queen of all Witches. There shall ye assemble, ye who would learn all sorcery, yet have not won its deepest secrets. To those I shall teach things that are as yet unknown.

And ye shall be free from slavery; and ye shall dance, sing, feast, make music and love, and let there be reverence and mirth—all in my praise. For mine is the ecstasy of the spirit, and mine also is joy on earth; for my law is LOVE UNTO ALL BEINGS. Keep pure your highest ideal; strive ever towards it; let NAUGHT STOP YOU OR TURN YOU ASIDE.

For mine is the secret door which opens upon the Land of Youth, and mine is the cup of the wine of life, and the Cauldron of Cerridwen, which is the Holy Grail of Immortality. I am the gracious Goddess, who gives the gift of joy unto the heart of wo/man. Upon earth, I give the knowledge of the spirit eternal; and beyond death, I give peace, and freedom, and reunion with those who have gone before. Nor do I demand sacrifice; for behold, I am the Mother of all living, and my love is poured out upon the Earth.

schools. The school offers instruction to solitary practitioners and to those who are interested in starting covens or worship communities of Wiccans. The publication of the Church of Wicca, *Survival*, is one of the longest-lived Wiccan newsletters in the United States. The organization is run just as one might expect a school and church to be run, although the requirements are a bit looser than for most accredited institutions. The Frosts teach or assist as requests come in. By their own admission, they have taken a perpetual vow of poverty in order to help other Wiccans to become educated in *the craft*. With the information gathered from the Frosts, anyone can become initiated and set up a Frostian-style coven or a coven of one's choosing.

The second group, The Church of All Worlds (or CAW), is a Neo-Pagan organization that contrasts in many ways with the Church of Wicca. CAW was founded by Otter (Tim) Zell and Lance Christie on April 7, 1962, after they had read Robert Heinlein's science fiction classic *Stranger in a Strange Land*. CAW has grown and morphed into a complex organization and now comprises several thousand members in the United States, Europe, and Australia. CAW is a unique combination of pagan, popular science, and science fiction sensibilities. Its adherents view the earth and all on it as one giant, organic organism, one Being. Humans are part of the cerebral-nervous system function of this great organism, which CAWers often call Gaia. The structure of CAW is understood to be organic and whole in the same fashion as the larger cosmos, which is seen as a great galactic womb.

There are three concentric circles in the CAW structure (members do not envision it as a hierarchy): Seekers, Scions, and Clergy. Each circle has three concentric levels distinguished by degree of training, learning, and commitment. Most members are Seekers and Scions. Simply visiting the CAW Website out of curiosity makes one a Seeker. Scions are individuals who have become CAW members. They pay membership dues and demonstrate commitment through service work and training or education and have dedicated themselves to building a local chapter of the CAW in their community. Three Scions in a location can apply to the CAW for consideration as a proto-Nest. If a proto-Nest successfully survives its first year and has increased in membership (by attraction, not promotion), it can be upgraded to a Nest. Several Nests in a given region are called a Branch, and these are served and overseen by Regional Scion Councils. The corporate headquarters of the Church of All Worlds is located in Toledo, Ohio, and has a board of directors who oversee all organizational, legal, and financial matters. There is a core group of Clergy (many of whom are located in California), individuals who have risen through the ranks by dedicated service and sacrifice.

Although this sounds very bureaucratic, there is, in fact, no overarching CAW theology or practice. The Church of All Worlds does sponsor a number of events and festivals at Annwfn, land owned by the Church, and these events allow members from different locales to come together and get acquainted. At the individual, proto-Nest, and Nest level, practices and/or beliefs are not dictated. Members can identify with Wicca or any number of other related Neo-Pagan faiths. Each Nest is free to organize its religious practices according to the needs and wishes of its members. The CAW has organized and sponsored many suborganizations. Among these is *The Green Egg*, the "official" organizational journal, which is widely known for its free-ranging and often rabble-rousing Forum section. Another is Nemeton, a music and recording company. CAW also features publications for parents, children, and young adults, as well as teaching guides for those who want to become Scions.

HOLIDAYS AND CEREMONIES

Most Wiccans adhere to an Eight-*Sabbat* Holiday cycle derived from a combination of Celtic and Anglo-Saxon sources. This cycle reflects the change of the seasons in the Northern Hemisphere and is divided into quarter and cross-quarter days. The quarter days are considered to be the true beginnings of each season, running from winter through autumn. Cross-quarter days are considered the middle or high point of each season and include the vernal and autumnal equinoxes (around March 21 and September 21) and the summer and winter solstices (around June 21 and December 21). Neo-Pagans who follow a pre-Christian European orientation generally observe a similar form of festival calendar. Some Neo-Pagans/Wiccans also observe the lunar cycles by celebrating the coming of the new and full moon. Neo-Pagans who draw their practices from Greek, Roman, or Egyptian sources will seek to enact rituals or festivals that were common to those peoples: for example, Roman hearth ceremonies and Egyptian dream rituals.

Neo-Pagans/Wiccans also have rituals for "handfasting" (betrothal and marriage), infant naming and consecration, funeral rites, and puberty rites of passage for young adults. Often, these ceremonies are conducted in an area that has been set apart for such purposes. If no such site is available, they take place in an area that has been set apart by a visualized "magic circle," which contains and consecrates even an ordinary room into a sacred space.

Magic may or may not be performed during holiday celebrations. Generally, magic is an activity that is largely independent of celebrations and is done in response to particular needs that come up (for example, if someone is going on a trip and wants a bit of protection on the road, or a family member is ill and seeks healing). Magic is a performance, a kind of ritualized prayer that seeks to align an individual with divine forces that can aid in achieving a desired outcome.

There are probably as many theories about magic among Neo-Pagans/Wiccans as there are Neo-Pagans. At its simplest form, magic is about getting the attention of a goddess or god or divinity in some way. The usual method is through a ritualized prayer. If a friend is ill, a Wiccan may choose a specific candle to represent that friend. Every day at the same time, he or she lights the candle and allows it to burn while chanting a prayer or invocation to a god or goddess of healing and visualizes the

Wheel of the Year

Samhain
October 31

Mabon
September 21

Yule
December 21

Summer

Winter

Lughnassad
August 2

Imbolc
February 2

Midsummer
June 21

Ostara
March 21

Beltane
May 1

The Wiccan "Wheel of the Year" is a cycle that reflects the change of seasons in the Northern Hemisphere. Divided into quarter and cross-quarter days, the Wiccan calendar is made up of eight holy days, including Samhain (Halloween), Beltane (May Day), and Yule (winter solstice).

friend healthy and happy. If a Neo-Pagan wants to eliminate a bad character trait or an unhealthy influence, he or she lights a candle or a small ritual fire and then writes down the negative character trait or the unhealthy influence on a piece of paper. Something personal can be added to the paper: a bit of scent or symbols that are significant to what is desired. There is often a stated declaration of what the paper represents: "On this paper, I write down all the things I must change and let go of, fear, anger, jealousy." Then the paper is folded or crumpled up and burned in the fire. As the paper is consumed, the Neo-Pagan affirms that as the paper burns and disappears, so shall the trait or unhealthy influence disappear. Such simple rituals of magic are often called *spells*. Often, Neo-Pagans/Wiccans develop highly individualized styles of doing magic. Diaries are important because they are a record of what works.

Magic rituals can be very simple or very complex. Whereas rituals for Holidays/Sabbats are generally formal and organized, rituals for magic are frequently conducted in communal surroundings with common objects. At formal holidays, many Neo-Pagans/Wiccans wear their best ritual robes or, in some cases, no robes at all. One creative ritual recently performed required an apron.

The most innovative magic ritual I've observed was intended to invoke the "spirit" of Betty Crocker (who is and has always been a fictional cultural American icon), for the purpose of assisting a crowded kitchen of six cooks to complete a baking project for a large Midsummer's gathering that evening. There was little room in the kitchen and even less time, and approximately six pies and three cakes had to be made. The High Priestess who was present and the owner of the kitchen, "drew the circle." This entailed going to each of the cardinal directions and invoking the element of that direction: "I call on the powers of. . . . East-Air (represented in this instance by a spatula), South-Fire (wooden spoon), West-Water (measuring cup) and North-Earth (chopping board)," etc. In the center she invoked "Betty Crocker" as the patron Goddess of Cooking, Decorum, and Good Manners, and implored her to assist the kitchen staff. The intent of the ritual was serious, the baking had to get done. Yet, the ritual itself was largely spontaneous and quite funny. It provided a focus, and it kept the atmosphere in a crowded, hot kitchen, light. The baked goods were the highlight of the event.

Very rarely do Neo-Pagans/Wiccans perform what might be called destructive or "black" magic that is manipulative or intends harm. Indeed, most Neo-Pagans/Wiccans are very careful about the magic they perform, often deliberating and discussing with others the possible effects before actually doing anything. Individuals who are found to be engaging in black magic are often shunned by the community and can be expelled from groups and organizations.

Large annual Neo-Pagan gatherings are held in North America, Europe, and Australia, and for many Neo-Pagans/Wiccans, these are regarded as special celebratory events. The Pan Pagan Festival (June), Heartland Spirit Pagan Festival (Memorial Day weekend), and DragonFest (July and August) often draw hundreds of individuals from all kinds of Neo-Pagan and Wiccan backgrounds for a weekend of workshops, dancing, drumming, shopping, rituals, eating, and relaxing. Pagan festivals are really the best places to get to know who Neo-Pagans and Wiccans are, what they think, and how they worship together. Some groups, such as The Church of All Worlds, conduct their own events. In addition to the larger festivals, there are many smaller regional or state events that occur on a more periodic basis.

GROWING UP, CHILDREN, AND FAMILIES

The American Neo-Pagan/Wiccan community is just entering its third generation. There are now whole families who have been following the ways of the Old Religion for up to forty years, despite the continuing prejudice of the wider society around them. As a result, children's literature to assist families in maintaining a Neo-Pagan/Wiccan household without the supportive structure of a central church or authority has developed. This literature focuses on how to instruct children about gods, goddesses, and rituals, and often includes information about gardening, cooking, and other survival and self-sufficiency techniques. Authors such as Silver Ravenwolf, with her Teen Witch series, have capitalized on the fact that there are many young Neo-Pagans/Wiccans who are attempting to forge and maintain their religious identities in a largely conservative Protestant Christian world. She encourages Neo-Pagan/Wiccan children to be cooperative with others while they defend their own religious freedom.

Neo-Pagan/Wiccan organizations such as the Gaia Community Center in Kansas City, Missouri, and the Circle Sanctuary in Wisconsin have developed specific programs and events for parents and children. Most large festivals have special workshops and program events for families. One young adult who was raised Wiccan recently stated that despite the prejudice that remains concerning witches, she cannot imagine having been raised any other way:

> The religion just suits me so well. How can I be sorry about being raised to appreciate nature and the seasons, of learning to see the Goddess in everything and everyone? How can that possibly be a bad thing? It's made me a more open person than many of my friends. I think I'm less afraid of things than they are.

CONTROVERSIES

Allusion has been made to common cultural prejudices concerning Neo-Pagans/Wiccans, particularly with regard to witchcraft and the practice of magic. Closely connected to this is the perception still found among many people that Neo-Pagans/Wiccans engage in Satanism, orgies, or black magic. As noted previously, Neo-Pagans/Wiccans are not well disposed to black magic. Furthermore, Neo-Pagans/Wiccans cannot worship something they do not believe in, and they do not believe in Satan. Claims about orgies are equally suspect. Most Neo-Pagans/Wiccans are tolerant of diverse sexualities and alternative relationships, but those who have their rituals generally agree that they have never seen an orgy. Some Wiccans, particularly those of the Brit-Trad lineage, practice their holiday rituals "skyclad" or nude. This is done only within the confines of private covens and is considered a mark of trust and intimacy among ritual participants. These rituals do not involve orgies. The body is considered a sacred temple of the god or goddess, and nudity is nothing to be ashamed of. All of this can be quite confusing for lay people. Unfortunately, the media tends to portray Neo-Pagans/Wiccans in stereotypical, sensationalistic ways, simply by playing off cultural preconceptions about religious minorities.

Neo-Pagans/Wiccans have had to fight for recognition of their religious practices at both the local and national level. Since the 1980s, there have been several attempts by conservative law-makers to rescind the tax-exempt status of already recognized Neo-Pagan/Wiccan groups. As recently as 1999, then-governor George W. Bush challenged the practice of Wicca on U.S. military bases: "I don't think that witchcraft is a religion. I wish the military would rethink this decision."[16] Some Wiccans have lost their jobs, housing, and even custody of their children, because employers or family members have used social prejudice against them to influence law enforcement and the courts.

In one recent case (2000), residents of a rural area adjoining land lawfully owned and utilized by a regional legally recognized Neo-Pagan organization attempted to rezone the property in order to drive the Neo-Pagans out. A number of incidental complaints against the Neo-Pagans who used the land were filed (they made noise, they practiced nudity, and allowed gay people on the property), but the main objection was simply that the Neo-Pagans existed and owned the neighboring land. When it was clear that the Neo-Pagan organization planned to get the ACLU and the national media involved, the neighbors abruptly dropped the case. Such attitudes have caused Neo-Pagans/Wiccans to be vigilant and defend themselves. Groups such as the Lady Liberty League, sponsored by Circle Sanctuary, serve as a legal clearing house, fielding cases filed on behalf of Neo-Pagans/ Wiccans and informing the pagan community at large about pending legal cases that might have a bearing on the rights of Neo-Pagans everywhere.

Additionally, a number of primers on Neo-Paganism/Wicca have been widely circulated to law enforcement agencies through-out the country. They explain what Neo-Paganism/Wicca is and differentiate such communities from those of Satanists. The best way to battle prejudices is, of course, through good information.

IN THE WORLD TODAY

Neo-Pagans and Wiccans have created religious traditions that are here to stay. Contrary to the view that Neo-Pagans/Wiccans are simply nostalgic "nature freaks," most are deeply committed to constructive and environmental technologies. Many are computer fanatics and any online search will display literally tens of thousands of Websites. Neo-Pagans/Wiccans were among the first religious folk to utilize computer bulletin boards in the early 1990s, and it is probably not too much of a stretch to speculate that they may have invented the first online virtual ritual. The larger Neo-Pagan/Wiccan community has always been and will probably remain very computer savvy, because it is the easiest way to keep in touch with others of like persuasion when there is no overarching authority or structure. Additionally, Neo-Pagans/Wiccans speak to an increased environmental sensibility and awareness of the earth as an integrated organism. Many Neo-Pagans/Wiccans have come to "the craft" largely because of a love of nature and a desire to see the great diversity of life on the planet respected and protected. Many are on the forefront of environmental movements. Despite a love of technology, they are also working on ways to simplify their own lives, reduce pollution, and teach their children how to be good stewards of Earth's resources. As the need for this kind of awareness grows, as it most surely will, Neo-Paganism/Wicca will undoubtedly attract more of the faithful to the fold.

9

New Kadampa Tradition

Every living being has the potential to become a Buddha,
someone who has completely purified his or her mind
of all faults and limitations
and has brought all good qualities to perfection.
Our mind is like a cloudy sky, in essence
clear and pure but overcast by the clouds of delusions.

—Geshe Kelsang, *Eight Steps to Happiness*

INTRODUCTION

In 1997, casual Western observers, particularly in Europe and New York City, were startled to learn that the seemingly unified face of Tibetan Buddhism, as embodied in the popular image of the Dalai Lama, was not as serene as it was frequently presented. A year earlier, the Dalai Lama and the Tibetan government in exile had issued several proclamations urging Tibetans not to pray to what seemed to be a minor and obscure Buddhist deity, Dorje Shugden. The proclamations were startling enough, coming from a figure who for many people around the world, even non-Buddhists, is widely regarded as the epitome of tolerance and compassion. What occurred less than a year later was even more startling. On February 4, 1997, the Director of the Institute of Buddhist Dialectics, Lobsang Gyatso, was found murdered along with two students, in private rooms in Dharamsala, India. The six individuals suspected in the murders were linked to Shugden worship (several of them had, in fact, left monastery life years before). At least two were known to have histories of intermittent violence and possible mental instability.

In the wake of these proclamations, a Buddhist school with prominent ties in England, the New Kadampa Tradition (NKT), began to vigorously protest the position of the Dalai Lama and to accuse him of attempting to undermine a legitimate Tibetan tradition. A group calling themselves the Shugden Support Committee (SSC) formed and began to protest against the Dalai Lama whenever he appeared at public gatherings, particularly in the West. The Dalai Lama and his government in exile in Dharamsala, India, were accused of destroying the monasteries and figures of Shugden, in much the same way that the Chinese destroyed such things when they invaded Tibet in 1959. Later, the Dalai Lama was accused of encouraging discriminatory practices against Shugden devotees, many of whom claimed that they had lost their jobs and seen their children expelled from schools for their faith in Shugden. The Dalai Lama and Indian officials denied these claims.

Suddenly, a deep chasm appeared to be dividing Tibetan Buddhism, and many Americans who had been drawn to this form of Buddhism found themselves in crisis. Although the New Kadampa Tradition and its teacher, Geshe Kelsang Gyatso, had been organizing for about twenty years prior to this public crisis, it had remained relatively unnoticed until this time. Now, taken aback, those who practiced Tibetan Buddhism began to ask many questions: What was New Kadampa about? What does it mean when Western scholars such as Robert Thurman referred to the New Kadampa Tradition as the "Taliban of Tibetan Buddhism?" Did New Kadampa have anything to do with the killings in Dharamsala? What was it about a minor Buddhist deity that could get both the Dalai Lama and the leader of New Kadampa so agitated that the former would try to ban its worship and the latter would openly defy that edict and accuse the Dalai Lama of attempting to destroy Tibetan Buddhist tradition?

This chapter will attempt to answer these questions as simply as possible. In the process, it will attempt to provide a glimpse of how complicated religious schisms can become and to show how a New Religious Movement was able to crack open a religious wound that has been festering in the heart of some Tibetan Buddhists for a little over a century.

FOUNDATIONS

The roots of the conflict between the Dalai Lama and the New Kadampa Tradition go back many centuries and involve components of Tibetan Buddhist practice that are far too complicated to fully explain in this brief chapter. To put it as simply as possible, the process of how Buddhism came to Tibet and how the Dalai Lama came to power involved delicate negotiations with powerful aristocratic families who ruled different regions of Tibet. These families were often connected to different schools of Buddhist practice.

The position of the Dalai Lama was established as part of a negotiated deal between these families and the Chinese emperor, and was understood to be both a religious and a political post.

TIBETAN SCHOOLS OF BUDDHISM

There are generally considered to be four principal and two minor schools of Tibetan Buddhism. Tibetan Buddhism is also known as Vajrayana Buddhism ("diamond vehicle" Buddhism), a reference to the emphasis on esoteric and tantric practice that is characteristic of Tibetan Buddhism.

Nying-ma (Ancient Ones) is traditionally considered the original Buddhism that first came to Tibet during the time of the Yarlong kings. In Tibetan tradition, the Buddhist teacher Padmasambhava was first invited to Tibet in the eighth century to teach the Dharma. This is a form of Buddhism that has been associated with the office of the Dalai Lama, although most Dalai Lamas have traditionally tended to perform Geluk practices. Kagyu (oral teachings) was founded by Khyungpo Nyaljar in the eleventh century. The emphasis in this school is on directed oral teaching and experience, and minimal text study. The visualization practices of Mahamudra were developed from Kagyu. Sakya was founded by the Khon family in the eleventh century under the leadership of Drokmi the Translator.

Geluk, founded in the fourteenth century by Je Tsongkhapa, is considered a synthesis school, in which the meditation techniques of all the previous schools are integrated with the teachings of *Highest Tantra Yoga* and the intellectual Buddhist philosophy of Nagarjuna. The Geluk school has dominated the office of the Dalai Lama for several hundred years.

Kadam is considered a minor school, traced to eleventh-century teacher Atisha. Atisha developed a sophisticated mind-training tool called *lojong*. These teachings have been very respected in the Geluk school, and so Kadam is often incorporated into Geluk. In fact, members of the Kadam school have often referred to the Geluk school as their "new Kadam," a possible source for Geshe Kelsang Gyatso's identification.

Rime is a nineteenth-century development. It is specifically eclectic, which means it openly combines all schools and methods together in order to maximize effectiveness. This school is most known for the large number of writers and poets it produced during the nineteenth century. Some members of the Geluk and Kadam schools have been suspicious of this trend. Rime is still considered a minor school.

The Dalai Lama was supposed to represent all the different schools of Buddhism in Tibet. Of course, these schools, attached as they were to individual powerful families, attempted to influence the Dalai Lama as much as possible. Over the years, one school, the Geluk, would come to dominate the office of Dalai Lama more than any of the others.

From time to time, successive Dalai Lamas attempted to moderate the power of the Geluk school. This led to conflicts that forced renegotiations between the Geluk school and the office of the Dalai Lama. The thirteenth Dalai Lama, Thubten Gyatso (the present Dalai Lama, Tenzin Gyatso, is the fourteenth), continued to question the dominance of the Geluk school. One result of his influence was that some Geluk monasteries in the Khams region of Tibet began to be influenced by other schools. Pabongka (1878–1941), a young charismatic Geluk teacher, saw this and became concerned. He began to move through the Khams area, teaching a kind of revivalist Geluk Buddhism in order to counter the introduction of other schools in the region. His Geluk teachings included the worship of a minor deity called Dorje Shugden.

Dorje Shugden is a "dharma protector," a kind of revenging guardian angel of a religious tradition. Dorje Shugden's main purpose was to protect the Kadampa subschool of Geluk from mixing with other schools of Buddhism. Pabongka was deeply convinced that his Kadampa school of Buddhism was the most original, correct form of Buddhism and could be traced directly to the great Buddhist teacher Atisha. He believed that Dorje Shugden should be employed to protect the Geluk school from being confused with the other schools. He had absorbed these Kadampa teachings, including the worship of Dorje Shugden, from his family and teachers. What was new and original about his position was his absolute conviction that this form of Buddhism was the most correct and pure form and that Dorje Shugden was the proper dharma protector to invoke to protect the Geluk school, even if that invocation had the potential for violence.

Pabongka succeeded in regaining the Khams region for the Geluk school and in the process, generated many brilliant,

BUDDHISM AND VIOLENCE

Buddhism is generally considered to be the least prone to violence of the great religions because of its principle of doing no harm, an ethic it shares with the Indian Jains. In the Buddhist Mahayana tradition, however, there are some rare exceptions to this belief. The example that is most often cited concerns a story that is told about one of the Buddha's previous lives. In one version of the story, the Buddha (in his life before he became The Buddha), was an enlightened young man who traveled on a ship with some other passengers. The captain of the ship was an angry, violent man who intended to take the possessions of the passengers and kill them all. The Buddha-to-be found out about this plot and determined that the man could not be dissuaded from his plan. The Buddha-to-be then decided to kill the captain to save the passengers and prevent the captain from accumulating any more bad karma. In a sense, the Buddha-to-be took on the karma of the evil captain himself and prevented the further destruction of all involved. He acted as a bodhisattva is to act—insuring that others can achieve enlightenment through him. Though his act caused him to be reborn in another physical life, the altruistic motive insured that he would be born as Buddha.

This story is often used by Buddhist teachers to demonstrate that one cannot always simply judge the exterior appearance of an action. It is also used as an example of extreme compassion. It is not used to justify any kind of personal action on the part of disciples; however, it is quite easy to see how someone could rationalize violent behavior by using this story. Dharma protectors are said to act in much the same way as the Buddha did in this instance. They remove obstacles and protect practitioners. In most cases, however, no individual practitioner is supposed to "act the part" of a dharma protector. One is to place trust in the dharma protector's ability to do its job. This being said, there are instances where Buddhists have operated as soldiers and rulers, roles that will always involve a certain amount of controlled violence. Ashoka, the Buddhist ruler of northern India in the third century B.C., was one such person. Various samurai families in Japan were also linked with specific Buddhist schools.

successful students. One of these was Trijang Rinpoche who later became the personal tutor of the present Dalai Lama and was very influential among the aristocratic families surrounding the Dalai Lama's court. Then, in 1959, the Chinese invaded Tibet. The Dalai Lama, as well as many millions of Tibetans fled to northern India, where they set up a government in exile. The old monastery system broke down and the Dalai Lama realized that his position had changed. Now, as he fought to regain his country and preserve the unique culture of an ancient people, he represented to the outside world not only all the schools of Tibetan Buddhism but all the people of Tibet as well. He decided that he had to "mix" individual schools of Tibetan practice in order to preserve all of them. In the early 1970s, the Dalai Lama began to publicly practice rituals and issue teachings from all the distinct schools of Tibetan Buddhism, including the Nying-ma school, the main rival of the Geluk. Furthermore, the Dalai Lama gave up his own practice of revering Dorje Shugden as taught to him by his tutor Trijang Rinpoche.

In 1975, a text called The Yellow Book began to circulate through Geluk communities. It contained an interpretation of Pabongka's teachings and stories about Dorje Shugden. It warned that dire things always followed Dalai Lamas who strayed from the path of Geluk and who mixed teachings. It is not known who wrote the book. The Dalai Lama was so upset about the text that he almost stepped down from his post, something no previous Dalai Lama had ever done. He felt deeply betrayed by the Geluk leadership. At the same time, many Geluk leaders felt deeply betrayed that the Dalai Lama was defying established convention and mixing the schools.

In 1976, the Kadampa teacher, Geshe Kelsang Gyatso, a recognized Tibetan mediation master who was a student of Pabongka's school and worshipped Dorje Shugden, was invited to give a series of talks in England. His sponsors liked him so much that they invited him to stay and he eventually established his Western school of Tibetan Buddhism there. At about the same time, the Dalai Lama began to urge those Tibetans who worshiped Dorje Shugden to give up the practice. This caused a deeper rift between him and some of the Geluk leadership. The practice of worshiping Dorje Shugden, while considered a relatively rare practice by a minor subschool, was still under Geluk jurisdiction.

Kelsang[17] built his following throughout the 1980s, and the rift between the Dalai Lama and certain Geluk leaders continued to grow. Finally, in 1996, the Dalai Lama made even stronger proclamations against the worship of Dorje Shugden and even implied, at least according to some, that he would deny worshippers of Shugden the highest Buddhist initiation of Kalachakra. This statement was in essence a declaration that he would deny such lamas "graduation" from a house of study that supported the worship of Dorje Shugden. The second stage of the conflict had begun. Then, in 1997, the murders in India occurred, followed by several other acts of attempted violence against individuals who supported the Dalai Lama's proclamations. By this time, Kelsang had established the New Kadampa Tradition as an enclave of Kadampa tradition in the West and there was no dismantling it. Today, the rift continues.

SCRIPTURES AND LEADER

New Kadampa Tradition does not so much have a specialized set of holy texts as it does an especially revered teacher, Geshe Kelsang Gyatso. Gyatso has labored tirelessly to translate and make available the Tibetan scriptures of the Sakya/Kadampa school for his students, which he augments with commentaries and interpretations. New Kadampa Tradition has organized its own publishing house, Tharpa Publishing, to make these texts available. For the most part, these books present Buddhist texts of the Geluk, Sakya, and Kadampa traditions without deviation. They represent the various methodological approaches of the Geluk tradition, including deity and guru generation practices, Lam rim, Mahamudra, and Higher Yoga Tantra.[18] Most recently, well-known philosophical works by the Tibetan master and Geluk founder Je Tsongkhapa have been translated and published with

Kelsang's commentary. All of this is in accord with standard Buddhist practice, and neither the texts themselves nor publishing them is especially unusual. The only new practices presented in New Kadampa Tradition are those that include revering Geshe Kelsang Gyatso as a living Buddha. This practice, not uncommon in Buddhist monasteries as carried out between guru and disciple, is called guru yoga. It is quite striking in a Western context. The difference can be found in Kelsang's commentaries. The texts are presented only within the context of the New Kadampa approach, which, according to Kelsang, is the purest, most traditional form of Tibetan Buddhism.

The other unusual aspect of Kelsang's teachings is the clear absence of any reference to the Dalai Lama or any other schools of Tibetan Buddhism. New Kadampa, as taught by Geshe Kelsang Gyatso, is presented as the Tibetan tradition that most truly and correctly transmits and translates Tibetan Buddhism to the

GURU YOGA

Guru yoga is essentially a devotional practice that involves a student completely merging himself or herself with the perceived greater self of the teacher/guru. The guru is generally taken to be a bodily manifestation of a greater being, such as a Buddha or bodhisattva (saint). By taking on or identifying oneself with the saintly or Buddhist nature of the guru, the student is encouraged to become like that saint or Buddha in essence. This process is often quite difficult for Westerners to understand, because it seems as if such individuals are sacrificing themselves in order to become like their teachers. Many Westerners are also cynical about the practice, seeing in it the potential for gurus to dominate students under their control.

In Buddhism, however, there is no real "self" that one is giving up. There is only one actual "Self" (Dharma-kaya) of which all people are expressions. There are also very strict rules that gurus are to follow in order to prevent abuse of their students, and then there is the Buddhist belief in karma, which holds that abuse of others will come back to the abuser. Although there have been instances of gurus abusing students, most Buddhist teachers have a pretty good reputation.

West. This is in line with Pabongka's insistence that a minority school of Tibetan Buddhism was/is, in fact, the most original, purest form of Buddhism. Indeed, if someone were introduced to Tibetan Buddhism through the New Kadampa Tradition, he or she could very well remain unaware that there are numerous schools and sublineages of Tibetan practice and that the Kadampa tradition was originally a minor branch of a regional school of the Geluk tradition.

Some criticism in the wider Tibetan community was originally tied to Kelsang when he began to publish some of the most revered Buddhist *yoga* practices, those that traditionally have been passed only from teacher to disciples. In recent years, perhaps in response to Kelsang's example, other teachers (including the Dalai Lama) have begun to publish similar practices (including the classic tantric practices of Chakrasambara and the Kalachakra initiation as practiced by both the Geluk and Nying-ma schools). Standard Buddhist practice insists on tolerance and minimal criticism of other teachers, therefore, the Shugden conflict has not overtly influenced the translations of or commentaries on traditional texts. For example, Kelsang's transmission of the Shugden *sadhana* and yoga in the text Heart Jewel does not comment upon the conflict between the Dalai Lama and certain Shugden devotees.

WORLDVIEW AND ORGANIZATION

From the time of Kelsang's original presentations in England until its official inception in 1991, New Kadampa Tradition has sought to become the largest Tibetan umbrella organization in the West. According to some, this strategy seems to be aimed at diminishing the effective power of the Dalai Lama as the official guardian of Tibetan Buddhism. Although New Kadampa officials are always quick to point out that they support a free and independent Tibet as much as anyone else, it is also clear that one of the goals of New Kadampa is a Tibetan Buddhism that can flourish without the necessity of returning to Tibet. It would exist, intact, in the West.

In this sense, Kelsang has come to regard the West (and the rest of the world beyond Tibet) as the place where the teachings of Tibetan Buddhism can best be safeguarded. Kelsang emphasizes that New Kadampa Tradition is the only Tibetan school that teaches the "true" Tibetan tradition, and New Kadampa Tradition claims that Kelsang is the first Tibetan lama to have truly adapted these teachings to meet the needs of Westerners. Additionally, according to New Kadampa Tradition, Buddhism is dead in Tibet and dying in India, implying that Kelsang and New Kadampa Tradition is Tibetan Buddhism's only hope. It is in this sense that New Kadampa Tradition has been accused of "fundamentalism" by some Western sympathizers of the Dalai Lama. Such an accusation does not do justice to the complex historical and political dimensions of this conflict, a struggle that is given greater urgency as Tibetans debate how best to preserve their unique religious heritage.

New Kadampa Tradition claims 4 million followers worldwide, although most observers maintain that these numbers are probably greatly exaggerated and that a membership of one hundred thousand to two hundred thousand is probably more accurate. There are only about 6 million Tibetans, and most of them are not Shugden worshippers. Because of Kelsang's original tie to his first British disciples, he has decided to make Great Britain the center of New Kadampa development. Official New Kadampa documentation claims that there are two hundred centers in the United Kingdom (U.K.) and fifty centers in Australia, Malaysia, Brazil, Mexico, the United States, and in continental Europe. Reportedly, there are also twenty-one residential centers in the U.K. with four hundred full-time residents. (Residential centers support branch centers or small localized meeting places, which might include private homes). All levels of practice are taught at branch centers, including simplified meditation and sadhana for children and young adults.

When a branch center is large enough, a property is purchased and an official center established. Each center is autonomous and is said to be spiritually joined to New Kadampa. The two principal officers are always New Kadampa members. The eventual aim is for New Kadampa to have a center in every British town.

PRACTICES, RITUALS, AND HOLIDAYS

As a form of Tibetan Buddhism, New Kadampa Tradition observes many of the same major rituals as other Tibetan schools, including the use of a traditional lunar calendar. The coming of a new year is generally observed on the full moon in January (for Mahayana Buddhists). The full moon in May celebrates the birth, enlightenment, and death of the Buddha. The full moon in March is celebrated as Avalokitesvara day, commemorating the *bodhisattva* (saint) in Tibet and China. There are also special annual commemorations for specific historical Buddhist teachers, such as Atisha (or Je Tsongkhapa), which are especially important in the Tibetan tradition. These festivals typically involve extended group meditation practices, followed by chanting, dharma talks given by important or noted teachers, drama and art presentations, and feasting.

Every year, Kelsang, like most Tibetan lamas, issues what are called "empowerments," or traditional meditation and teaching sessions that culminate in students being initiated into specific, often more advanced, practices. Most of these empowerments occur at annual Kadampa Festivals, which are generally held once a year in each country with a large New Kadampa following. After being empowered, a student has permission to practice special forms of meditation or devotional prayer called sadhanas ("directed disciplines"). Accumulating and becoming proficient at these practices/empowerments, some of which can be quite complicated and take hours or days to perform, is part of how one establishes credentials toward advancement in the system of Tibetan Buddhism.

The particular practice of invoking or worshipping Dorje Shugden is a beginner's sadhana and is part of learning the process of guru yoga. Dorje Shugden is said to be a manifestation of the great Tibetan bodhisattva Manjushri, and New

Kadampa literature provides a traditional Buddhist history of the lives of Dorje Shugden in order to establish his holy lineage. Students are to depend on Dorje Shugden to protect their practice and to prevent obstacles from getting in the way of their becoming fully enlightened Buddhists. Furthermore, Dorje Shugden helps spread the good news of Geluk/New Kadampa Buddhism by generating wealth, fame, and healing to his worshippers. This emphasis on worldly abundance is a little unusual for a dharma protector, but in and of itself, it is not necessarily controversial.

One thing that sets Dorje Shugden practice apart from other Buddhist teachings is a section of the sadhana ritual that was composed by the charismatic Pabongka. This passage, usually read metaphorically by New Kadampa Tradition practitioners, has apparently been taken quite literally by some Shugden supporters in India. It reads in part: "Now exhort to violent actions, Shugden, who is the main war-god of Dzong-ka-ba's tradition and its holders, the angry spirit. . . . In particular it is time for you to free [or kill] in one moment the enemies of Dzong-ka-ba's tradition. Protector, set up your violent actions without letting your previous commitments dissipate. Quickly engage in violent actions without relaxing your loving promises. . . . Quickly accomplish these actions that I entrust to you, for I do not have any other source of hope." [19] These violent actions are intended to be performed by Dorje Shugden himself, as an act of retribution against those who would mix Geluk teachings with any others. They are not intended for humans to perform. Some question the distinction and wonder what might occur if a disciple felt sufficiently threatened and very strongly identified with Dorje Shugden through the practice of guru yoga. These are the questions that both New Kadampa Tradition and other Tibetan Buddhist practitioners have to confront.

CONTROVERSIES

Within the Tibetan Buddhist community, now a worldwide community that includes several thousand Westerners, the rift between New Kadampa, other Shugden worshippers, and the Dalai Lama has caused great anguish. It is seen as a breakdown of Tibetan unity, and some fear that the schism could damage the prospects of the Tibetan people regaining their homeland anytime soon. China has made much of this conflict, accusing the Dalai Lama of religious intolerance. Chinese officials have claimed that the Dalai Lama relies on the utterances of astrologers (reportedly, it was one of his astrologers who originally encouraged him to speak against the worship of Dorje Shugden). Indeed, they argue that the entire incident proves that Tibetans are a primitive, irrational people who need to be modernized and civilized. Tibetans and Western observers who are critical of New Kadampa Tradition have argued that the position of Kelsang and the SSC plays into the hands of Chinese propaganda, and have even accused SSC members of being agents of China (There is no substantial proof of this).

In spite of speculation, no connection has been found between New Kadampa Tradition and the murders in Dharamsala. In fact, Kelsang has expressed deep concern over the incident. He has condemned the killings and has encouraged Shugden devotees to act as true Buddhists by working toward compassion and nonviolence. For the time being, both sides have backed off. It remains to be seen how, and if, the schism may be resolved in the future.

Apart from the political controversies, New Kadampa Tradition has faced some of the same obstacles that many New Religious Movements confront. New Kadampa Tradition, as taught by Kelsang, emphasizes a semimonastic approach, which often involves making a choice to live apart from relatives in sequestered communities. Again, this is a common practice in Tibetan culture but can be perceived by Western families as appearing "cultish." Some families in England have accused New Kadampa Tradition of brainwashing relatives and of asking them to give up their possessions. It is true that New Kadampa Tradition does ask for donations in a manner that is not traditional Buddhist practice, but this is a Western practice, and since New

Kadampa Tradition is working within a Western framework, it can hardly be blamed for adapting accordingly.

Obviously a large income is needed to accomplish the task of establishing a mission or center in every English city, and although no one is forced to do anything, devotees are encouraged to give interest-free loans and donations of money or property. There have apparently been instances where loans received have only been paid back if individual donors insisted on reimbursement. According to British officials, some members of New Kadampa residence centers have "gone on the dole" (applied for government unemployment assistance) to help finance themselves and centers; however, this practice is not encouraged or condoned by the New Kadampa organization. At least as far as can be determined, Kelsang's role in the development of his school appears genuine. There are no reports of him accumulating money or property for himself; all income appears to go to the New Kadampa organization. Furthermore, although there are some dissatisfied former members of New Kadampa Tradition, many more say they have found great fulfillment in these Buddhist practices and are dismayed that the Dalai Lama has singled out their teacher and his teachings for exclusion from the greater body of Tibetan Buddhism.

IN THE WORLD TODAY

New Kadampa Tradition is quickly becoming a schismatic movement of Tibetan Buddhism, pursuing an independent line of tradition, and initiating its own teachers/lamas without the approval of the Dalai Lama. As one scholar puts it, "The Dalai Lama believes Dorje Shugden is an earthly god. Kelsang believes it is a manifestation of Buddha,"[20] and therein lies the seeds of conflict. There are some who see this as a tragedy threatening Tibetan unity; others, including Kelsang, apparently see this process as an inevitable consequence of differing views regarding how the future of Tibetan Buddhism may best be secured. Since China's invasion of Tibet, many lamas have come to see the West as a repository of *dharma* teachings. Indeed, one of the first lamas to bring Tibetan Buddhism to a Western audience (Chogyam Trungpa Rinpoche) once stated that although the invasion of Tibet was an event of great and terrible hardship, there was the equally great blessing of his being able to participate in sharing the cultural wealth and beauty of Tibetan Buddhism with Western disciples.[21] Many Tibetan lamas have shared this view, and Tibetan Buddhism has become one of the fastest growing forms of Buddhism in the West. Both the Dalai Lama and Kelsang are successful Buddhist teachers, each with his own following. Both have contributed immensely to the popularity of Tibetan Buddhism in Western societies. It is a testament to both sides in this conflict that the rhetoric has eased and that those involved seem to be taking seriously the Buddhist admonition that, with restraint and compassion, time itself sometimes presents a solution.

10

New Religious Movements in the News

Humankind will make a leap forward
if it can take a fresh look at itself and the universe,
changing its rigid mindset.

— Li Hongzhi, *Zhuan Falun*

The public oftentimes becomes aware of New Religious Movements only when one of them becomes destructive. This chapter discusses three New Religious groups that have distinguished themselves by doing something spectacular and dangerous and have made headlines in the last fifteen years. They are not the only religious groups to have self-destructed in recent history, but they are among the best known. The accounts presented here are not exhaustive; more detailed summaries can be found in studies that are available in print and online. The point of this chapter is to provide some guidance about what it is that might make some New Religious Movements destructive as well as to reinforce the fact that the vast majority of New Religious Movements have not been and do not become destructive. The chapter also discusses the positive role that New Religious Movements can play in society.

BRIEF PROFILES OF THREE INFAMOUS
NEW RELIGIOUS MOVEMENTS
Branch Davidians

On April 19, 1993, after a fifty-one-day siege, which began on February 28, FBI and ATF (Bureau of Alcohol, Tobacco, and Firearms) agents stormed the Branch Davidian complex at Mount Carmel, located approximately eight miles beyond the city limits of Waco, Texas. There remains much controversy surrounding the sequence of events leading up to the fire that raged through the complex of buildings immediately after the assault on April 19.

The leader of the Branch Davidians, David Koresh, believed that events leading to the end of the world would center on Mount Carmel, the site of the Branch Davidian complex. He had originally prophesied that the end would come in 1995, but the arrival of the FBI and ATF agents on February 28, 1993, for the official purpose of issuing a warrant, changed his assessment. The warrant was related to illegal weapons that were reportedly on the property. Although it is true that there were weapons at the Mount Carmel complex, it is also a fact that several members of the community bought and sold weapons at gun shows, a practice that is not at all uncommon in rural Texas. That a few illegal gun components would later be found is also not uncommon. Government claims of a huge weapons stash, however, have not been substantiated.

There has been no firm conclusion about what caused the massive fire that quickly engulfed the buildings. Initially, the government claimed that the Branch Davidians had placed fuel or items containing fuel (such as lanterns) around the complex in order to ignite them should the government attack. This conclusion has come under scrutiny for several reasons, including the fact that many of the members obviously died of gunshot or stab wounds, which would make the simultaneous lighting of multiple fires both superfluous and difficult to coordinate. In addition, survivors have quite adamantly denied that there was any overall directed suicide plan. There have also been charges that ATF agents knowingly utilized a flammable tear gas at the time of the attack. In any event, David Koresh and about seventy-five members of the Branch Davidian community, including twenty-one children, died—killed by suicide, homicide, and the effects of smoke and fire. Eight members escaped but several were badly burned.

The Branch Davidian community began as a religious movement that had broken away from the Seventh Day Adventist Church in the 1930s. David Koresh, formerly Vernon Howell, had risen in the ranks to become the leader of the community by the mid-1980s. By all accounts, he was a gifted speaker with an extraordinary ability to memorize whole portions of the Bible. The Branch Davidians regard David Koresh as a messiah, a prophetic leader appointed by God to issue in the End of Days (the second coming of Christ). (However, Koresh did not claim to be Christ returned.) Under his leadership, the Branch Davidian community began to prepare for the End of Days and to expect a conflict with government forces. Koresh initiated a plural marriage practice in his community and began to exercise tight control over community activities at this time. There were charges of child abuse and statutory rape, which remained unsubstantiated even after an investigation by Texas Child Services, an organization that was not empathetic to the Branch Davidian community. Children who had left the site prior to the fire showed no evidence of abuse. Despite charges that Koresh was a tyrant in the group, most followers remained loyal to him and still do. Survivors insist that although he wanted group cohesion, he did not force anyone to do anything they did not want to do. They add that the proof of this was that his control of information flow on and off the property was not very good and that he allowed individuals to leave the property in March and April.

One of the most tragic aspects of the Branch Davidian case was revealed by subsequent investigation into FBI and ATF activities. These investigations uncovered that although both agencies retained the professional services of religious studies experts, they actually heeded the advice of psychologists and *anticultists* who insisted that the potential for loss of life was minimal. This advice contradicted information given by religious studies scholars, some of whom had been in contact with David Koresh himself and had warned government agents that treating the Branch Davidian situation like any other hostage event could end in tragedy. Government agencies chose to ignore these recommendations and even denied Koresh the opportunity to speak to religious scholars that he had met with and trusted. The FBI and ATF did not take the religious dimensions of the conflict seriously and most religious scholars agree that if they had, this tragedy might well have been avoided. There remain approximately thirty-five to forty Branch Davidians worldwide, and they vary widely in their theological interpretations of the events. Bonnie Howell, Koresh's mother, has expressed the belief that her son died for a reason that will be made clear at a future time.

Aum Shinri Kyo
On March 20, 1995, members of the Japanese faith community Aum Shinri Kyo (The Supreme Truth) released a lethal nerve

gas, sarin, into a commuter car at a Tokyo subway station. Twelve people died and almost five thousand were wounded in the attack. Experts now agree that had the attack been better coordinated, the number of deaths could easily have numbered in the thousands. Aum Shinri Kyo members had already attempted at least nine biological attacks in various locations by spraying germ and biological toxins, including anthrax, from buildings. The Japanese legislature and U.S. Naval Installations were among the intended targets. None of these agents were administered in sufficient amounts to cause harm. Members of the Aum Shinri Kyo leadership have also been responsible for several murders, including the death of Japanese broadcaster Tsutsumi Sakamoto and his family. Sakamoto, who was well known for being critical of Aum Shinri Kyo, had interviewed several movement members, and it is believed he and his family were targeted because of the potential damage the interview may have caused once broadcast.

Aum Shinri Kyo was founded by the prophet Shoko Asahara, formerly Chizuo Matsumoto, who was born partially blind but had become an acupuncturist and yoga teacher. In the early 1980s, he traveled to the Himalayas and studied Hinduism and Buddhism. He also became obsessed with the Book of Revelation in the New Testament and the prophecies of sixteenth-century Christian prophet Nostradamus. His complex blend of yoga, Eastern philosophy, and Western millennial beliefs led him to form Aum Shinri Kyo in 1987. At its peak, the faith community had about twenty-thousand members worldwide, most of them in Japan. Asahara stressed strict community discipline and predicted that great world disasters were coming, a result of the crass materialism and war technologies that were engulfing the world. Through his dietary, yoga, and meditation practices, he also promised that his followers would be able to achieve super-human abilities. He was a charismatic, prophetic figure, and his followers came to believe that he was Christ. He became convinced that government forces in Japan and the United States would try to prevent his group from advancing the cause of the return of Christ, so he decided that Aum Shinri Kyo members should attempt to protect themselves by preemptive attack. The membership began purchasing property, equipment, and biological/chemical agents for this purpose.

Following the sarin attack, more than one hundred members were arrested and charged. The trials were expected to last more than a decade. Kazuaki Okazaki, one of the founding members of Aum Shinri Kyo, was sentenced to death for planning the killings of Tsutsumi Sakamoto and his family and the death of a former Aum Shinri Kyo member in 1999. Despite the arrests and convictions, the Japanese legislature was unable to ban the group. In 2000, Aum Shinri Kyo was reorganized by Rika Matsumoto, the third daughter of Asahara. Under her leadership, the group changed its name to Aleph. The adoption of the name Aleph initially caused great controversy, because it is a popular name used by many businesses in Japan. On April 24, 2003, prosecutors demanded a death sentence for Asahara, who had refused to answer questions during his last two hearings. This is where the situation currently stands.

Heaven's Gate

Beginning on March 23, 1997, and continuing in three successive phases, thirty-nine members of the UFO faith group, Heaven's Gate, systematically committed suicide by taking a lethal combination of phenobarbital and vodka. Some of the members found at the suicide site, an exclusive house in Santa Fe Rio, California, were found with plastic bags tied over their heads, partially suffocated. Each was dressed identically in Nike tennis shoes and a black jumpsuit. A tag identified each of them as being of the "Away Team." The group believed they were liberating themselves from their bodies, which were only "temporary containers," and that they were going to be "beamed up" to a waiting space ship. The suicides coincided with Easter and with the closest approach of the comet Hale-Bopp to the earth. The timing led some to conclude that the group had become convinced that a space ship was accompanying the comet, a speculation that had been popular on UFO radio shows in the weeks leading up to the incident. Other evidence supports the view that the leader of the group, Marshall Applewhite, seemed to regard the appearance of Hale-Bopp more as a sign that the time of the group's "translation to a level above human" had come.

Marshall Applewhite (also called "Do" or, as he referred to himself, "The Present Representative") had been a religious leader for over twenty years, when he and his flock made their momentous decision. In the 1970s, Applewhite and his spiritual, platonic partner, Bonnie Lu Trusdale Nettles, gained modest notoriety for founding an earlier UFO faith community, Human Individual Metamorphosis (HIM), in 1975. They traveled around the country and adopted rather humorous names for themselves, such as "Bo and Peep." Their followers called them "The Two." Eventually, they adopted the names "Do" and "Ti" (positions on the musical scale). The Gospels in the New Testament, The Book of Revelation, and various science fiction narratives, including *Star Trek* and *Stranger in a Strange Land*, provided their principal inspiration. Do and Ti believed that the human body, with its desires and impulses, was a limited container that trapped the infinite possibilities of the soul. Extraterrestrials represented a superior form of life, and it was possible for disciplined humans, who systematically denied their desires for sex, too much food, and other luxuries, to escape their bodies and be "grafted into" the advanced body of an alien. Ti died of cancer in 1985. Do founded another group after Ti's death. Called Total Overcomers Anonymous (TOA), this group was later reorganized into Heaven's Gate. Do gradually became convinced that political and governmental forces would seek to prevent his community from advancing to a higher level. He believed that the present Earth would be recycled, because it was being controlled by evil forces and was beyond any redemption.

Heaven's Gate members lived a strictly celibate, monastic-style communal life and supported themselves by supplying web-design services through a company called Higher Source. Eight of the male members, including Do, had voluntarily submitted to testicular castration in order to stop sexual urges. Many of the members had lived highly successful lives prior to joining the group; some had left their families behind. Members were free to come and go at any time, and in fact, several members left the group after the suicides occurred. Prior to the suicides, Do produced a number of video tapes in which he explained his philosophy regarding the "coming action." All members of the group also recorded a videotaped message, explaining why they were choosing to leave their bodies and saying goodbye to their families. These materials were sent to a former member who no longer lived with the group. He called the authorities shortly after receiving the materials to alert them to the suicide plans. Subsequent to the initial suicides, two other former members, who had not been present at the house, also committed suicide in a similar fashion, both hoping to join their brothers and sisters at the promised higher-than-human level.

WHAT MAKES A NEW RELIGIOUS MOVEMENT SELF-DESTRUCTIVE OR DANGEROUS?

When events like this occur, all the experts rush out and try to explain why and how such things can happen. One question at the heart of these explanations is whether there is a common denominator in these groups that creates the conditions for violence or self-destructive behavior. Many theories have been proposed and some seem to have merit. For example, each of the groups described above fostered millennialist expectations; they expected the world to end soon. Each group was also led by a male, charismatic prophet who sought to create a separate environment for his followers and feared the corrupting influence of the outside world. Each group, through the leader, was convinced that external forces, generally seen as "the government" would either attack them or try to prevent the group from fulfilling its mission.

The difficulty with the above analysis is twofold. First, there are many religious groups and movements and even mainstream organizations that fit this description. Pat Robertson's 700 Club is a case in point. His group believes deeply in the imminent ending of the world, and Robertson is a charismatic, well-spoken male minister. While Robertson's organization is too large for it to segregate its membership from the world, one of his messages has always been that Christians need to separate themselves from dangerous influences. He frequently seeks to draw distinctions between true believers and those who are astray or evil. Finally, Robertson often alludes to government or social forces that he believes will attempt to ensnare Christians or thwart the Second Coming. Despite these beliefs, there is no indication that Robertson and his religious organizations are in any way physically dangerous or self-destructive. Thus, simply having these beliefs is not enough.

Secondly, focusing only on what these three groups had in common obscures the real differences among the groups and what the conditions were that led to their respective destructive behavior. Heaven's Gate and the Branch Davidians were small groups with limited membership and a highly segregated lifestyle. Koresh's group self-destructed only after a siege that lasted almost two months and after they had been attacked. The events unfolded in a poor, rural part of Texas that had become the focus of heavy government and media attention, and the Branch Davidians were convinced that they were being threatened by satanic forces. Members of Heaven's Gate self-destructed as a result of their own free will, quietly, in a very wealthy and exclusive California neighborhood. They made sure that they would not be disturbed or prevented from attaining their goal of leaving this life. In fact, from the standpoint of the Heaven's Gate membership, their actions were not destructive at all—they were liberating. These are two very different reasons for self-destruction. In addition, both groups had been around for many years, and no one could have accurately predicted (particularly in the case of Heaven's Gate) that the end would come in the manner it did.

Aum Shinri Kyo presents a different picture. It was a much larger movement, numbering more than twenty thousand members.

Complete segregation of such a large group is impossible to achieve, and the group chose to attack others rather than to self-destruct. Furthermore, only the close immediate leadership, a group of about one hundred, participated in acts of violence. Although rank and file members might have contributed money or resources, they were not personally involved in the planning or execution of the sarin attack. In this case, the group itself did not self-destruct; only the leadership was responsible for acting out the deadly fantasies of the leader.

This analysis suggests that there are more differences than similarities among these three groups, yet many people continue to regard them and their activities as virtually identical. One reason for this may be the spectacular and unusual ways in which each group acted upon its principles. The fire at the Branch Davidian complex was certainly a horrifically impressive event. It was captured live on television after tensions had been built up for several days while everyone waited to see what government agents would do. The mass suicide of the Heaven's Gate membership was also shocking and sensational, particularly because it occurred just after members of another (unrelated) group, *The Order of the Solar Temple*, had committed suicide in Canada. The sarin attacks, perpetrated by Aum Shinri Kyo, certainly merited media attention, especially as the potential number of killed and wounded was averted not by medical or police attention but by the number of mistakes the attackers had made.

Many scholars and individuals who are part of the anticult movement have drawn up a list of dangerous characteristics or warning signs that they believe lay people and authorities should watch for when assessing the potential for violence or self-destruction of New Religious Movements. In their warnings, they include some of the following questions: Does the group want you to contribute all your possessions? Does the group/leader teach a rigid doctrine of exclusivity (that is, do they think that only they have the Truth)? Does the group/leader encourage members to break the law? Some experts even ask, "Does the group have a sense of humor about itself or its doctrine?"

The difficulty with these questions is that under these criteria, many mainstream religions and political ideologies could easily be considered dangerous or cultish. Early Christians and Latter-day Saints often contributed and/or shared all of their possessions. Anabaptist Christian groups such as the Hutterites still do. Most religions can be quite rigid about their core doctrines and most maintain that they have the edge on truth. Jesus is recorded as having broken Jewish law any number of times, and both Gandhi and Martin Luther King, Jr., insisted that an unjust law should be resisted and broken. Finally, according to some Branch Davidians and according to the pre-suicide recorded messages of Heaven's Gate members, laughter and happiness were present in both communities. Heaven's Gate members saw their bodies as so silly and useless that they saw no reason not to get rid of them. Oddly enough, a religious leader like Southern Baptist Jerry Falwell is rarely seen to crack a smile when a doctrine that he holds dear is on the line.

Given these contradictions, it seems rather difficult to determine precise warning signs according to the parameters established by anticult scholars and others. Perhaps the problem is that these individuals do not focus on features of New Religious Movements that are truly warning signs. For example, it may be more constructive to look for warning signs in the dynamic (not the beliefs) of the group(s) or in the relationship between the group and the outside world, including political and government agencies. Furthermore, if a group says its members are going to self-destruct, then they might actually be headed that way. There are often other definite warning signs. Marshall Applewhite of Heaven's Gate had issued several proclamations detailing the group's preparations for departure. The Aum Shinri Kyo sarin project took months to plan and what its leader (Asahara) was doing was never secret. Records of his preparation were left all over Japan. David Koresh repeatedly warned that if government agents attacked Mount Carmel, they would not prevent the Branch Davidians from fulfilling their purpose in God. The point, in each case, is that the utterances

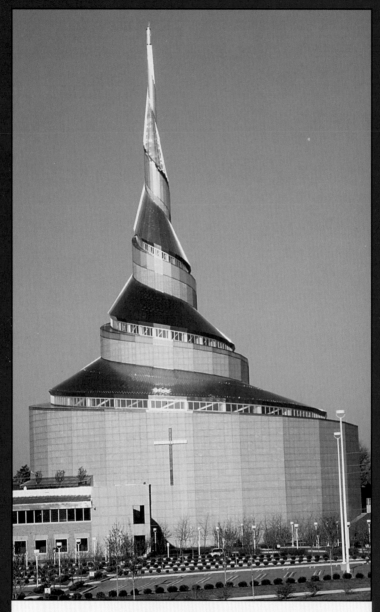

In 1994, the Community of Christ Temple was dedicated in Independence, Missouri, and serves as world headquarters for this religious organization. More liberal than the Latter-day Saints, the Community of Christ is very active in mission work and claims approximately 250,000 members in 40 countries.

The Baha'i faith has approximately 5 million members, including 84,000 adults in the United States. The Universal House of Justice, located in Haifa, Israel, is the principal legislative body of the Baha'i movement. Since 1963, nine representatives of the faith have met at the Universal House of Justice to resolve difficulties, oversee mission work and outreach, and determine how the Baha'is will respond to national and international issues of concern.

Aimee Semple McPherson, the founder of the Foursquare Gospel Church, celebrates her twenty-fifth anniversary as an evangelist at Angelus Temple, Los Angeles, California. According to McPherson, Foursquare represented the four aspects of Jesus Christ as the Savior, The Baptizer with the Holy Spirit, The Healer, and The Soon-Coming King.

Rael, formerly Claude Vorilhon, founded the world's largest organized international UFO religious group, the Raelians, in 1975. Raelians promote an atheistic and scientific worldview and hold that a superior species known as Elohim created humans. Raelians openly embrace nonlethal technology and science, believing that human beings simply need to learn how to utilize technology responsibly for the betterment, rather than the destruction of life.

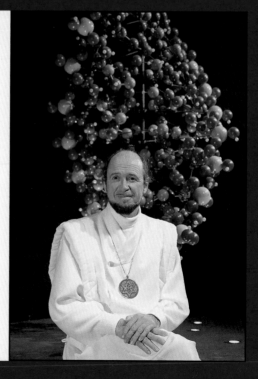

Thirty-nine members of the UFO faith group Heaven's Gate took their lives in late March 1997, during the comet Hale-Bopp's closest approach to Earth. Some believed that the group, led by Marshall Applewhite, thought that their bodies were only "temporary containers" and that their souls were going to be "beamed up" to a spaceship hiding behind the comet. Others supported the theory that Applewhite saw the appearance of Hale-Bopp as a sign that the time of the group's "translation to a level above human" had come.

The Yoruban orisha Eshu is the messenger god of the crossroads, the gatekeeper, and must be contacted first at the beginning of each Ebbo—a ritual that consists of an offering, songs, and prayers, and is performed to resolve conflicts or straighten the balance of the universe. This shrine figure is part of the Paul Tishman collection of African Sculpture.

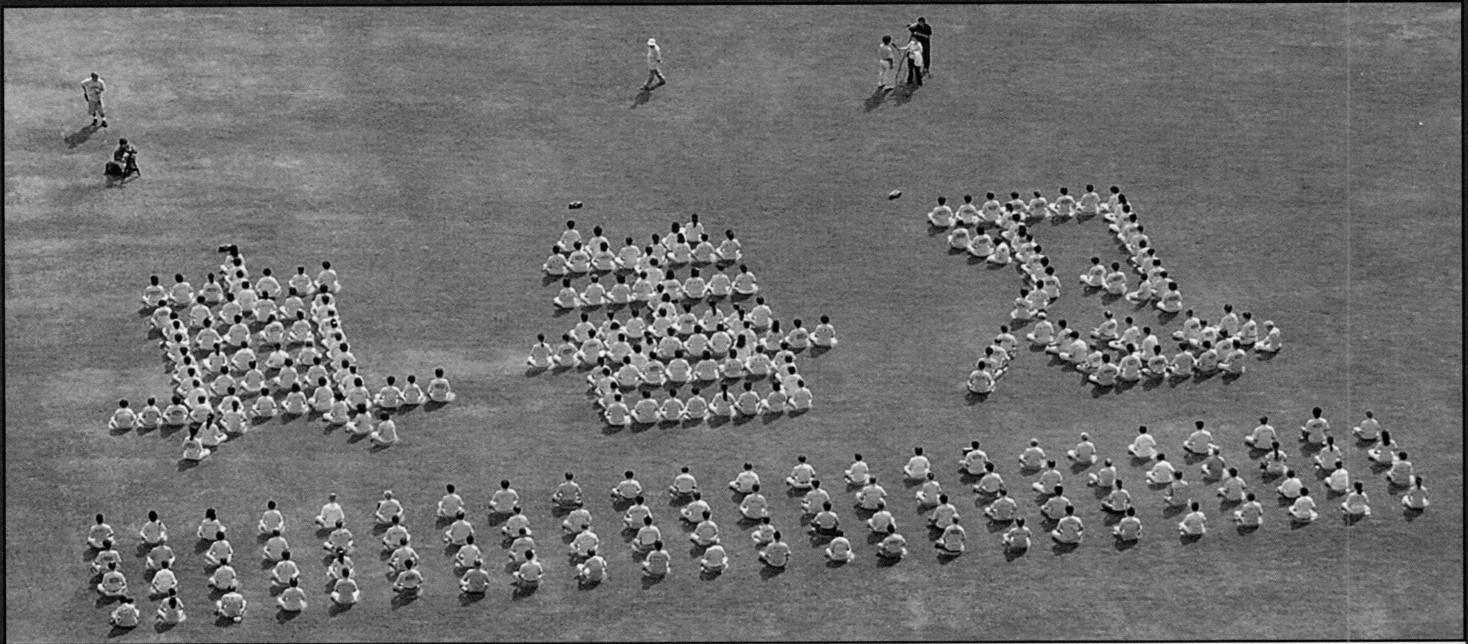

Falun Gong, or Falun Dafa, is a Chinese spiritual movement that promotes the improvement of mind, body, and spirit, while combining elements of Buddhism and Taoism with its own set of moral and ethical teachings. Shown here are members of the Falun Gong spelling out the Chinese characters (left to right) for "truthfulness, benevolence, and forbearance" in Victoria Park, Hong Kong, during "World Falun Dafa Day," May 13, 2003. In recent years, the Chinese government has viewed the group as a cult and has persecuted them.

The Pentagram, a common Neo-Pagan/Wiccan symbol, represents the four natural elements: earth, air, fire, and water plus spirit. Neo-Pagans/Wiccans strive to come into harmony or unity with nature and are generally nature worshippers.

and announcements of religious groups, particularly those who believe that they may be under attack in some way, need to be taken seriously. Furthermore, the only way to take a New Religious Movement seriously is to find out about it, no matter how odd or different the beliefs or how seemingly offensive the leadership of such a movement may be.

The relationship between New Religious Movements and political structures or government agencies also needs to be considered. Destructive group violence never occurs in a vacuum. In each case mentioned above, government forces were believed to be attempting to harm or thwart the purposes of the religion. Although this may seem paranoid, there is a long history of government opposition to New Religious Movements, either for religious or political reasons. The Baha'is challenged the religious doctrines of Iranian Islam, and the Latter-day Saints threatened the absolute authority of the U.S. government in its project to facilitate the settlement of the West. Both groups were openly attacked by government authorities who sought to destroy membership loyalty by imprisoning leaders and seizing property. The Chinese government has persecuted members of Falun Gong in the same fashion. Orisha worshippers and Wiccans have had to take their religious concerns to Congress and the Supreme Court to guard against lawsuits and harassment by their neighbors. The records of early Christians, Muslims, and Buddhists contain many accounts of government persecution. Jews have suffered great indignities because of their religious culture.

The second part of the equation of self-destruction lies within the cultures out of which New Religious Movements emerge. It lies within each of us. Cultures, like individuals, are forced by New Religious Movements to consider the nature of political and religious loyalties, and this is sometimes a painful and uncomfortable exercise. Furthermore, there is no one set of characteristics to look for in a New Religious Movement that can, in and of itself, determine whether it may become destructive. It is also unlikely that the vast majority of New Religious

Movements will become destructive in the manner of a Heaven's Gate or an Aum Shinri Kyo.

Currently, there are almost 2,700 religions in the United States, most of which are New Religious Movements of one kind or another. Given these numbers, self-destructive activities, such as those committed by members of Heaven's Gate, appear to be quite rare. Similarly, New Kadampa Tradition should not necessarily be viewed as violent simply because a few Shugden worshippers in India took it upon themselves to serve as dharma protectors. In a moment of real fear, a group of Latter-day Saints took it upon themselves to massacre 120 men, women, and children at Mountain Meadows in 1857, and yet this by no means indicates that we should conclude that all Latter-day Saints are so inclined. The vast majority of New Religious Movements and their members are nonviolent; only a few go astray.

Nearly all the religious movements detailed in this book have suffered through controversy and have come out the other side, stronger, better organized, and able to continue. It is this strength, this ability to come through obstacles that should be considered the most positive element of New Religious Movements and their membership. Mainstream churches, synagogues, and mosques are established, entrenched institutions in their cultures. There is nothing wrong with this—such features are measures of stability—but certainly, even entrenched institutions can have their moments of crisis and controversy. Individuals who start New Religious Movements and the members who follow them are often spiritual seekers. They are not simply crazed fanatics who brainwash others into becoming fanatics. Such people are often not satisfied with the answers they have been given by culture or by their birth religion(s). They may have questions that are not being answered, or they may not fit the established norms. Oftentimes, the leaders of New Religious Movements are individuals who are motivated by experiences or feelings of injustice, and they want to solve the problem, whether it is poverty, suffering, alienation from society, pollution, illness, or government exploitation. They have to struggle with themselves, and often with powerful exterior forces, to maintain their beliefs and practices. It is important to remember that Jesus, the Buddha, and Muhammad are considered to have been such people.

Individuals like Rael, Joseph Smith, Baha'u'llah, and Li Hongzhi are believed, by their followers, to have found answers to some of life's most perplexing problems. The Latter-day Saints are living out the legacy of Smith's vision that Christ's restored Kingdom on Earth entails that one of the functions of the Church is to care for and support all its members. Baha'u'llah envisioned a world where religious and racial conflict could be solved in a Universal House of Justice. Rael speaks directly to the social and personal uncertainties and discomforts attending biogenetic research. Li Hongzhi has challenged the absolute authority of the Chinese government by encouraging Falun Gong members to believe in their own internal authority. It is conceivable, then, that although people may not agree with the solution that each prophet or New Religion suggests, the value of the issues and questions they have raised remains valid. The leaders and members of New Religious Movements have their own lessons to teach us. Let us listen and learn from them.

Chapter 2: The Church of Jesus Christ of Latter-Day Saints

1805   Joseph Smith, Jr., is born on December 23, in Sharon, Vermont, the fourth child of Lucy Mack and Joseph Smith.

1820   God the Father and Jesus Christ appear before a fourteen-year-old Joseph Smith, Jr., and explain to him that all revival churches are corrupt and he should wait for God to reveal a plan.

1823   Angel Moroni visits Joseph in his bedroom three times in one September night; these visitations are part of a series of lessons that culminate in Smith's retrieval of the golden plates buried at Cumorah.

Nineteenth Century
Santeria (Orisha worship) spreads throughout Caribbean and southern United States

1805
Joseph Smith born in Vermont

1893
Baha'i faith first comes to United States

1890
Aimee Elizabeth Kennedy, founder of Foursquare Church, born

CE (AD)

1800   **1850**   **1900**

1830
Book of Mormon first printed

1846
Brigham Young chosen to lead Latter-day Saints

1844
Siyyid Ali Muhammad founds what would later become the Baha'i faith

1862
U.S. Congress passes Morrill Anti-Bigamy Law

1827 Smith finally retrieves the plates, said to be written in Reformed Egyptian; with the assistance of a device called the Urim and Thummim and God's inspiration, Smith translates the plates and generates what later becomes The Book of Mormon.

1829 John the Baptist appears to Smith in May and gives him the Aaronic Priesthood and his scribe Oliver Cowdery; this restores the apostolic priesthood that was said to have been lost when Jesus died and ascended; later in the summer, apostles Peter, James, and John restore the lost Melchizedek Priesthood in a similar fashion.

1949
Gerald Gardner publishes
High Magic's Aid

1968
First Wiccan church
founded in the United States

1963
The Universal House
of Justice is established
in Haifa, Israel

1993
U.S. Supreme Court rules that
Church of Lukumi Babalu
Aye can practice in Florida

1992
Li Hongzhi, the
founder of Falun Dafa,
introduces his teachings

1950   **1970**   **2000**

1973
Claude Vorilhon (Rael) is contacted
by an extraterrestrial and founds
Raelian movement two years later

1976
Geshe Kelsang Gyatso begins to garner
a New Kadampa following in the West

1979
Rael begins plans to build embassy in Jerusalem

1997
Rael founds
Clonaid

1999
Falun Gong
demonstrate
in Beijing

1830 The Book of Mormon is first printed by the Grandin Print Shop in Palmyra, New York; on April 6, the Church of Christ, Smith's first organization, assembles as the restored Church of Jesus Christ on Earth.

1831 The Church of Christ (Mormons) moves to Kirtland, Ohio, and achieves a peak membership of almost 3,200 people, nearly the population of Cleveland, Ohio, at the time.

1832 The Church of Christ (Mormons) begins mission work in Independence, Missouri.

1833 Smith publishes sixty-five of seventy-one additional revelations received from God in a collection called The Book of Commandments; after much revision, these revelations become the basis of Doctrine and Covenants.

1834 The Church is renamed and becomes The Church of the Latter-day Saints.

1835 It is likely that the secret practice of polygyny may have begun around this time.

1838 Smith takes his flock to Far West, Missouri; a few members stay behind in Kirkland, Ohio; the Church adopts its official name: The Church of Jesus Christ of Latter-day Saints.

1838–1839 Latter-day Saints are harassed by their neighbors in Missouri; some are massacred while others are driven out of the state.

1839–1840 Smith begins to resettle his people in what will become Nauvoo, Illinois; at this point the Church has almost seventeen thousand members.

1843 The revelation concerning polygyny is officially received, even though according to Doctrine and Covenants 132, Smith had been aware of God's teachings concerning the practice for over a decade; the practice was not openly announced until 1852 and was not consented to by the community until 1880.

1844 Smith becomes the mayor of Nauvoo, Illinois, which has grown to become the second-largest city in the state after Chicago; on June 7, William Law, who has become disaffected from Smith, exposes the practice of polygyny and charges that Smith teaches that there is more than one God; the allegations are written in a local newspaper, *The Nauvoo Expositor*; on June 10, Smith, acting under a claim of authority as mayor, has the press, office, and printed copies of the paper destroyed; June 25 through 27, Smith and his brother Hyrum are arrested and held in jail in Carthage, Illinois; a mob attacks the jail on June 27 and kills Joseph and Hyrum.

1846 Brigham Young is chosen to lead the Latter-day Saints to a desert valley located in what was then Mexican Territory; Young becomes the second president of the Church and the community founds the city that will become Salt Lake City, Utah; the Saints arrive at the valley of the Great Salt Lake in 1847.

1851 Pearl of Great Price is first published; in 1880 it is declared scripture.

1852 The practice of polygyny is formally announced at a Latter-day Saints meeting.

1857 On September 11, a coalition of Saints and Kiowa Indians, led by Bishop John D. Lee, attacks and destroys a wagon train of 120 men, women, and children who they think are connected with a contingent of federal forces that have been dispatched to attack and subdue the Saints; this event is now called the Mountain Meadows Massacre.

1860 Reorganized Church of Jesus Christ of Latter-day Saints is officially established at Amboy, Illinois, with Joseph Smith, III, as president; LDS membership reaches almost 61,000.

1862 The U.S. Congress passes the Morrill Anti-Bigamy Law, making plural marriage illegal.

1880 Doctrine and Covenants 132, authorizing polygamy, is confirmed by LDS membership.

1882 Congress passes the Edmunds Act, which exacts heavy penalties for practicing plural marriage; the practice continues in secret.

1887–1890 Congress rescinds the corporation of the LDS Church by passing the Edmunds-Tucker Act; despite constitutional challenges, the federal government begins to seize the assets of the Church; when the Supreme Court upholds the legislation, Congress moves to strip all Saints of their citizenship.

1890 In September, LDS President Wilford Woodruff announces the principle of the "Great Accommodation" and declares that all Saints should cease the practice of plural marriage; his manifesto does not reject or amend Smith's previous revelation contained in Doctrine and Covenants 132—it simply suspends the practice; LDS membership stands at 188,000.

1978 On September 30, the Priesthood makes an Official Declaration that allows all worthy members in the Church to hold the Priesthood; this pronouncement allows African and African American males to hold those positions; the Church unanimously agrees to the Declaration.

1995 LDS has an estimated membership of slightly more than 9 million.

Chapter 3: The Baha'i Faith

1844 On May 23, in Persia (Iran), Siyyid Ali Muhammad assumes the title "The Bab" (meaning "the Gate"); he announces that his purpose is to herald the coming of the "Promised One" of all religions; his followers become known as Babis; it is said that 20,000 of his followers were martyred, and his movement caused great tumult.

1850 The Bab is executed as a threat to Islam.

1863 Hussein Ali-i-Nuri, an important follower of The Bab, confides to his fellow believers that The Bab had all but declared him to be the "Promised One"; on April 21, he begins to declare his station openly and assumes the name Baha'u'llah, the title that The Bab was said to have used for him; Baha'u'llah was imprisoned for much of his life, first in Baghdad, then Istanbul, and finally in Akkar, Syria; prior to his death, he appointed his son Abdu'l-Baha as his spiritual successor.

1892 Baha'u'llah dies and the spiritual leadership of his movement passes to Abdu'l-Baha.

1893 The Baha'i faith is first brought to the United States through African American converts.

1900 The first American Baha'i community house is organized in Wilmette, Illinois.

1908 Abdu'l-Baha is released from prison; he arranges for the remains of The Bab to be brought from Persia and interred near what is now Haifa, Israel.

1921 Abdu'l-Baha dies, leaving his grandson Shoghi Effendi as the trusted Guardian of the revelation of Baha'u'llah.

1957 Shoghi Effendi dies suddenly, leaving a body of commentaries and instructions that allows for the structural organization of the international Baha'i community to continue; at this time, several splinter Baha'i organizations split from the main body because of differences over succession of the Guardianship.

1963 The Universal House of Justice, the governing body of the main Baha'i movement, is established in Haifa, Israel, near the site where the bodies of The Bab and Baha'u'llah are buried.

Chapter 4: The Foursquare Gospel: A Pentecostal Church

Nineteenth Century "Holiness" movement emerges out of revivalist Methodism; it emphasizes a baptism of the Holy Spirit with resulting gifts of the spirit, such as speaking in tongues, prophecy, and healing.

1890 Aimee Elizabeth Kennedy is born on a Canadian farm.

1901 On January 1, in Topeka, Kansas, Charles Fox Parham leads a Bible study on the first day of the twentieth century; one of his students, Agnes Ozman, is "taken" by the Holy Spirit, and her experience of speaking in tongues leads Parham to specific theological conclusions about the power of the Holy Spirit to heal and bestow supernatural linguistic abilities; this event is generally considered to be the birth of modern Pentecostalism.

1905 In Houston, Texas, African American preacher William Joseph Seymour hears Parham preach and is inspired to take the message of immediate healing and salvation to Los Angeles where he begins the Asuza Street Movement; the movement fuses African American worship styles with white holiness doctrine, and the basics of Pentecostal worship develop.

1908 During the initial spread of Pentecostalism, Aimee Kennedy is exposed to the doctrine at a revival meeting led by Robert Semple; Aimee and Robert marry.

1910 The Semples travel to China to found a mission church; Robert dies after contracting malaria.

1912 Aimee Semple returns to the United States, marries Harold McPherson, and tries to live a normal life.

1915 During a critical illness, Aimee Semple remembers her initial calling and asks for God's healing; after her recovery, she begins to organize and lead her own revival church; her husband Harold takes care of the children.

1918 Harold leaves Aimee to her evangelizing mission.

1922 During a particularly intense revival in Oakland, California, Aimee Semple McPherson has a vision that leads to the foundation for the Foursquare Gospel Church; she establishes the Angelus Temple in Los Angeles, California.

1944 After successfully establishing her church, Aimee Semple McPherson dies; her son Rolf assumes leadership of the Church until 1988.

2001 The combined world membership of the International Foursquare Church is estimated at 5 million people in 141 countries, with a total of about 38,000 individual churches.

Chapter 5: Raelians: A UFO Religion

1973 On December 13, Claude Vorilhon reports his encounter with an Eloha, an extraterrestrial who appoints Vorilhon to be the Elohim's prophet to the rest of humanity; Vorilhon receives the name Rael.

1975 Rael founds the Raelian movement.

1979 Rael is directed by the Elohim to write letters to seven famous rabbis to reveal that the messiah is close and that the Embassy in Jerusalem must be built.

1989 In May, Rael delivers his first public addresses in Israel.

1990 Under the direction and with the permission of the Elohim, Rael changes the Raelian medallion out of respect for the victims of the Holocaust.

1991 Rael makes a formal request of the state of Israel to begin building the Embassy for the Elohim.

1992 In January, after the Raelians make two requests, the Chief Rabbi of Israel acknowledges the request and places the matter "under study."

1993 On March 25, after sending out press releases, Rael announces that he is the Messiah (Moshiach); he does this at the Wailing Wall in Jerusalem; Chief Rabbis from New York and Israel deny his claim. Following these events, the Raelian movement is investigated by Israeli security and determined not to be a threat; Raelians hope with anticipation that their request will finally be heard. On December 9, then-acting Israeli Prime Minister, Yitzak Rabin, replies to the Raelians that Israel cannot honor their request. On December 13, the coming of the Elohim for this twentieth anniversary was indefinitely postponed due to the failure to secure a site for the Embassy; as the Raelians put it, "Regrettably, peace has been postponed."

1997 Rael founds Clonaid, the human cloning research and service facility.

2001 First attempts of human cloning are reportedly made.

2002 Rael announces first successful cloning of humans; several announcements of subsequent clonings have been made, none confirmed, all controversial.

Chapter 6: Orisha Worship: Ifa, Santeria, Candomble, and Lukumi

Sixteenth Century Yoruban peoples develop their traditional religion, which they refer to as "Ifa" because of the central role of the Ifa divination practice.

Early Sixteenth–
Nineteenth Century Many Yoruban people are taken captive in the Western slave trade and brought to the Americas; most are taken to Brazil in South America and later to the Caribbean, Cuba, and parts of the southern United States; they take their religious beliefs and practices with them; Ifa mixes and blends with Native American, other African and Catholic religions, taking on regional and national forms, such as Santeria, Lukumi, and Candomble.

Nineteenth Century Santeria begins to take distinctive shape in Cuba and gradually spreads to other islands in the Caribbean and to the southern United States, particularly in Florida and Louisiana.

1930s Candomble is organized in Brazil; it was not practiced openly until the 1970s.

1959 Oseijeman Adefunmi relocates from Nigeria to Cuba and becomes one of the first Africans to be fully invested in the priesthoods of both Africa and Cuba; he founds the African Theological Archministry, Inc.

1970   The African Theological Archministry, Inc., establishes the Kingdom of Oyotunji in South Carolina as a living environment in which to preserve African cultural and religious traditions from Yorubaland.

1993   U.S. Supreme Court rules that the city of Hieleah, Florida, may not prohibit the Church of Lukumi Babalu Aye from performing its traditional forms of animal sacrifice; this sets a precedent that leads to a greater openness about Ifa-Lukumi-Santeria practices in general.

Chapter 7: Falun Gong (Falun Dafa)

1992   Li Hongzhi, the founder of Falun Dafa (the original name of the movement), originally introduces his teachings through the Qugong Research Association of China.

1996   After withdrawing his school from the Qugong Research Association, Li relocates to New York State; his movement is reportedly growing rapidly in China and beginning to concern local officials.

1996–1998   The Chinese government steps up persecution of various religious movements in order to bring their followers under control.

1999   On April 25, in response to the government crackdown, ten thousand Falun Gong practitioners demonstrate for "freedom of practice" on the site of the 1989 democracy demonstrations, Tiananmen Square; in July, Falun Gong/Falun Dafa is declared illegal by the Chinese government.

2004   The Chinese government has declared that the Falun Gong movement is under control; it is believed that up to one thousand persons may have been imprisoned, tortured, or killed; Falun

Gong practitioners have been vigorously attempting to place their situation before the court of international public opinion.

Chapter 8: Neo-Paganism and Wicca

1884 On June 13, Gerald Brosseau Gardner is born in Lancashire, England.

Winter 1888 Young Gerald is shipped off to Nice, France, in the care of a nanny; because his family is in the shipping business, he later travels to and lives in Portugal and the Canary Islands; Gerald is exposed to many things on his travels, including spiritualism, literature, and occultism; he is tutored but has to educate himself because his family's mobile lifestyle is not stable enough for him to attend school.

1900 At the age of 16, Gardner goes to work on the Elkington tea plantation as an apprentice planter; the Elkingtons dabble in mysticism and the occult.

1902–1905 In 1902, Gardner takes a job as a planter on the Nonpareil Estate tea plantation in Ceylon (now Sri Lanka); Gardner's father purchases a nearby rubber plantation and makes Gerald the manager, but he continues to work on the tea plantation.

1905–1908 Gardner returns to England and joins the Legion of Frontiersmen, a private militia; he hooks up with relatives who are interested in spiritualism; he also becomes involved in Freemasonry at this time; he finds out that his grandfather, Joseph Gardner, had been involved with witches in Scotland.

1908–1916 Gardner's father sells the rubber plantation; Gardner travels back and forth from Singapore and Malay to England as his money and job offers fluctuate because of war and economic changes; he comes down with black fever and malaria several times; when he is in Singapore and Malay, he stays with indigenous island peoples and studies their native ways; he also studies books on English and Celtic mythology and folklore.

1921 *The Witch Cult in Western Europe* by Margaret Murray is published; text causes a sensation in the anthropological and literary worlds because of its premise that the original European religion was a goddess-worshipping culture that was wiped out by Christianity during the Burning Times (the Inquisition) and that remnants of this ancient pre-Christian tradition survive.

1926 Gardner is appointed inspector of the licensed opium shops in Singapore; he has taken up amateur archaeology, and studies the many occult texts that are being published by Aleister Crowley and theo-sophical societies.

1927 Gardner returns to England, falls in love, and gets married; he studies spiritualism and does research on Welsh and Basque mythology and folklore.

1931 Margaret Murray publishes *The God of the Witches*, a sequel to *Witch Cult*.

1932–1935 Gardner continues to work for the British foreign service; he travels in Egypt, Palestine, China, and Vietnam (known then as French Indochina); publishes a book on Malaysian magic and folklore; and continues to study spiritualism but concludes that most spiritualists are frauds.

1936–1947 Gardner and his wife settle on an estate and join or investigate several occult fraternities and nudist organizations; after retiring in 1936 (at the age of

52), he takes up "naturism" (nudity—at nudist clubs) on the advice of his doctor; Gardner meets many important individuals, including occultist Aleister Crowley, who will influence his work.

1948   *The White Goddess* by Robert Graves is published; it will be very influential for a generation of Wiccans to come.

1949   Gerald Gardner publishes *High Magic's Aid*, which includes his early version of an initiation rite; by this time, Gardner may have been initiated into a magical coven by a woman named Dorothy Clutterbuck (or Old Dorothy); accounts as to when this occurred vary widely.

1951   Gardner splits with Clutterbuck's coven and organizes his own; there is also some evidence that it is by this point that he begins to travel and teach.

1953   On Midsummer's Eve: Doreen Valiente is initiated into Gardner's coven and is quickly made High Priestess.

1954   Gardner publishes *Witchcraft Today*, which is an essential statement of his religion of Wicca.

1956–1957   Tabloid newspapers in England publish sensationalistic articles linking Gardner's Wicca with Satanism (an accusation that started early and has stuck); these allegations are investigated by Doreen Valiente.

1958   Gardner publishes *The Meaning of Witchcraft*; the book includes Doreen Valiente's refutation of the connection between Wicca and Satanism; Valiente leaves Gardner's coven and sets up her own.

1959–1971   American Ray Buckland makes contact with Gardner; through Valiente and others who Gardner has initiated, Gardnerian-style covens begin to multiply;

Alex Sanders (initiated into a Gardnerian coven in 1967) finds an original copy of the Gardnerian Book of Shadows and embellishes its contents; later, he initiates Janet and Stewart Farrar.

1962 Tim Zell and Lance Christie are inspired to create a Neo-Pagan organization based on Robert Heinlein's science fiction classic *Stranger in a Strange Land*.

1968 Gavin and Yvonne Frost found the first Wiccan church in the United States.

1972 Wicca is given tax-exempt status as a legitimate religion for the first time in the United States; a more detailed chronology can be found at *http://www.cyprian.org/Articles/gardchron.htm.*

Chapter 9: New Kadampa Tradition

Eleventh Century According to New Kadampa Tradition teachings, the tradition is established by the great Buddhist teacher Atisha.

Early Twentieth Century Pabongka leads a revivalist Kadampa movement in the Khams region of Tibet in order to reestablish dominant Geluk practice; one of his students, Trijang Rinpoche, becomes a favored tutor of the present Dalai Lama.

1959 China invades and occupies Tibet, forcing the Dalai Lama and several million Tibetans into exile.

Early 1970s The Dalai Lama begins to speak against the worship of Dorje Shugden and to openly mix other schools of Tibetan practice, including Nying-ma.

1975 The Yellow Book, a text critical of Dalai Lamas who mix practices, is disseminated among Tibetan Buddhists.

1976 Geshe Kelsang Gyatso, a recognized Kadampa lama and Dorje Shugden worshipper, is invited to England to give a series of classes; he begins to build a following in the West.

1984 The Dalai Lama reiterates his proclamations against Dorje Shugden.

1991 New Kadampa Tradition is officially organized as an umbrella Tibetan Buddhist institution.

1996 The Dalai Lama issues even stronger proclamations against Dorje Shugden and hints that he might deny its practitioners the ultimate initiation of the Kalachakra; New Kadampa Tradition followers begin to protest the Dalai Lama's stance, issuing challenges to the Dalai Lama and making charges of discrimination against Shugden devotees.

1997 Three students of the Dalai Lama are murdered in Dharamsala, India; the murders are traced to Shugden worshippers but not to New Kadampa Tradition.

NOTES

CHAPTER 4:
The Foursquare Gospel: A Pentecostal Church

1 *http://www.foursquare.org/index.cfm ?cat=about&subcat=history.*

2 Ibid.

3 Ibid.

CHAPTER 5:
Raelians: A UFO Religion

4 Theosophy was a movement that began in India during the 1870s and was started by a woman named Helena Blavatsky. She intended it to be a synthesis of Western and Eastern religion, philosophy, occultism, and mysticism as well as science. She claimed that her information was obtained through a group of "ascended masters," some of whom were nonphysical and communicated with her in trance. She was also said to be influenced by a collection of mystical ancient poems called the Stanzas of Dzyan. Her followers went in many directions after her death, and in various forms, theosophy is probably the single most influential doctrine underlying many New Age ideas. Spiritualism is the spiritual and religious idea that dead and other nonphysical beings can be contacted by living beings still in the physical realm. This idea first became popular in the United States during the mid-1840s.

5 *www.rael.org.*

6 Claude Rael, *The Final Message.* (Norwich, U.K.: The Tagman Press, 1998), 90.

7 Claude Vorilhon, *Extraterrestrials Took Me to Their Planet.* (Brantome, France: l'Edition du Message, 1986), 283.

8 *www.rael.org.*

CHAPTER 7:
Falun Gong (Falun Dafa)

9 *http://religiousmovements.lib.virginia .edu/nrms/falungong.html.*

10 The swastika is a symbol that predates Nazi use and is found in practically every ancient religious or mythological system. It is almost always a positive symbol that designates the power of the sun, the seasons, or the energy found in the body or in nature. This is true whether it is spinning counter-clock-wise or clock-wise. Swastikas are frequently found in Buddhist and Hindu artwork and often represent the turning of the wheel of dharma or history. The function of the Nazi swastika was very different. Nazi artists tilted the swastika so that it fit into a diamond rather than a square. Unfortunately, the use of the swastika by the Nazis has probably adversely affected this universal and ancient symbol for many years to come.

11 Li Hongzhi, Appendix I, *Zhuan Falun.* 20 April 1994. Available online at *http://www.falundafa.org/book/eng/flg.htm.*

12 Berend ter Haar's online scholarly discussion of Falun Gong at *www.let.leidenuniv.nl/bth/falun.htm.* Some of the best work on Falun Gong has been done in the Netherlands and through CESNUR, an Italian based resource group on international New Religious Movements operated by Massimo Introvigne at *www.cesnur.org.*

13 Bodhisattvas operate rather like saints in Roman Catholic Christianity. Avalokitesvara is one of the most popular bodhisattvas and is known as Kuan/Quan Yin in China. One of his or her attributes is having a thousand arms or hands, all of which are reaching out to assist others.

14 *http://www.trincoll.edu/depts/csrpl/ RINVol2No3/Falun%20Gong.htm.*

CHAPTER 8:
Neo-Paganism and Wicca

15 Carol Matthews, "Witchcraft and Neo-Paganism," in *America's Alternative Religions* (New York: SUNY Press, 1995).

16 *http://www.positiveatheism.org/writ/ bushwicca.htm.*

CHAPTER 9:
New Kadampa Tradition

17 Kelsang is an appropriate name to use in this instance. Although the name Gyatso could be used, the Dalai Lama's personal second name is also Gyatso and this might be confusing. The term *Geshe* is a title, rather like "doctor of divinity," and cannot be used as a proper name in this instance.

18 Lam rim, Mahamudra, and Highest Tantra Yoga are Buddhist meditation and ritual techniques of gradually increasing sophistication and difficulty. Lam rim teachings are considered very basic to the development of bodhicitta ("open heart") and are generally taught when a follower has taken the bodhisattva vow (that is, they have vowed to become saints, leading all other beings to nirvana before entering it themselves). The Lam rim (stages on the path to enlightenment) teachings are said to have been taught by the first Kadampa sage, Atisha. Mahamudra and Highest Tantra Yoga are much more advanced ritual meditation practices and are generally attained by only a few practitioners, although New Kadampa Tradition made the texts of these practices available, for the first time, to a wide public audience. All these forms of meditation were developed into a single system by the Geluk master and scholar, Je Tsongkhapa. They were then passed down to all Geluk schools, including the Kadampa.

19 This translation can be found in an article written by Georges Dreyfus in 1999 for the Tibetan government in exile at *http://www.tibet.com/dholgyal/shugden-origins.html*. The New Kadampa Tradition translation of this prayer to Dorje Shugden can be found in Geshe Kelsang Gyatso's text *Heart Jewel: Sadhana and Guru Yoga of Dorje Shugden*.

20 *http://www.tibet.com/dholgyal/CTA-book/chapter-5-4.html*.

21 As noted by Chogyam Trungpa Rinpoche during a dharma talk given after his Kalachakra initiation in 1983 and witnessed by the author.

ache/ashe—Life energy that is believed to circulate throughout the cosmos. It can be accumulated in certain people, places, or things. Orishas control and focus ashe.

anticultists—Anticultists are a movement of their own in many respects. Some of them are members of Christian organizations, and others consider themselves to be simply concerned citizens. Although there is great variety in their approaches, most anticultists see New Religious Movements as potentially dangerous. Most of the rhetoric about brainwashing and the deceptive practices of cults is derived from anticultist literature. The Cultist Awareness Network (CAN) was the organization that advised the Bureau of Alcohol, Tobacco, and Firearms regarding the Branch Davidians. They are also the group that first labeled the Branch Davidians a cult, even though the group had been present in the Waco, Texas, area for at least two decades. Anticultists are also largely responsible for the development of deprogramming procedures that have occasionally been used on individuals against their will, at the direction of distressed family members, to reverse effects of alleged brainwashing. This procedure has itself come under attack, and many anticultists have suspended the practice. In 1999, the Church of Scientology, which had been pursued by CAN for years, sued CAN and took over its assets.

Awo—A person in Ifa who can perform many of the rituals and divination practices for individuals needing them. An Awo is not as powerful or important as Babalawo.

Babalawo—Literally "father of secrets"; this is the highest priest title in Ifa. A Babalawo can perform all divination and ritual practices, except for a few reserved for women priestesses, and generally acts as a community elder.

bata drums—These are traditional double-headed drums that are used in festivals to call the Orishas to possess humans.

bodhisattva—Enlightened being with Attainment Status in the Buddha School who is higher than Arhat but lower than Tathagata.

charism/charisma—Greek term for a "gift" or "a grace." It was commonly understood to be a special talent or ability that an individual was simply granted by the gods. Early Christians and Pentecostals interpreted the term to mean abilities exhibited by individuals when they are under the influence of the Holy Spirit (speaking in tongues, healing, prophetic gifts, wisdom, etc.).

Christian Perfectionism—This Holiness doctrine maintains that the experience of being saved or sanctified completely removes the possibility of conscious sin. An individual can still sin unknowingly (out of ignorance, for example) but cannot commit sin by choice, because his or her nature has been completely cleansed and reborn. It is a controversial doctrine that is not shared by all Christians.

Contactee Movement—This refers to the large numbers of individuals who claimed to have had contact with extraterrestrials during the 1950s and early 1960s in the United States. Some of them went on to found UFO religions. There have been a few notable contactees since then, of which Claude Vorilhon/Rael is one.

coven—A small group of Wiccans (witches) who regularly meet to celebrate Wiccan holidays and life events (births, deaths, marriages) or to study. It can be understood as a home church for nature worshippers.

The Craft—This is a term that Wiccans use to describe the totality of their religious practices. Their religion is something that they help to create and form and is valued as much for the beauty of its content as it is for its utility and flexibility. The term is believed to come from Freemasonry and was incorporated into Wicca by Gerald Gardner.

Dafa (dah-fah)—The "Great Way," or The "Great Law"; short for the practice's full name, Falun Dafa, "The Great (Cultivation) Way of the Law Wheel."

dan (dahn)—Energy cluster that forms in the bodies of some cultivators in internal alchemy; in external alchemy, it is referred to as the "Elixir of Immortality."

dan-tien (dahn-tyen)—"Field of dan"; a field located at the lower abdominal area (Falun Gong).

Dao (dow)—"The Way" (also spelled "Tao").

dharma—For Buddhists, the term generally refers to the teachings of the Buddha, given by the Buddha for the enlightenment of all beings. These teachings can include meditation, visualization and psychological techniques, physical exercises, rituals, or texts that enable students to reach enlightenment.

Dharma Body—Li Hongzhi claims each person who receives his teaching becomes capable of turning the Dharma Wheel that exists in them (the Falun). And since he has activated this through his teachings, his power also increases as each follower's power increases. Therefore, he is able to provide protection for his followers through his increase of power.

Dharma Wheel—The Buddha was said to have "turned the wheel of Dharma," which means he helped bring the world into a new period of teaching. In Western terms, it is similar to when Christians speak of a "new dispensation" or a new period in church history.

drawing a circle—This is the ritual act of making a common space (like a kitchen or living room) into a sacred space, where magic or ritual can be performed.

Ebbo—A task, ritual, or work that is often assigned as a result of a reading. A worshipper will go to an Awo for advice about a healing. The Awo will do a reading to determine the nature of the illness and assign an Ebbo. The Ebbo will normally include a series of rituals, prayers, and offerings to a particular Orisha.

Eguns—These are the ancestors. Everyone has them. They watch over, interact with, and attempt to influence the actions of the living. Occasionally they have to be acknowledged, and the Orishas can assist in this process.

Falun (fah-luhn)—"Law Wheel."

Falun Dafa (fah-luhn dah-fah)—The "(Cultivation) Way of the Law Wheel."

Falun Gong (fah-luhn gong)—"Law Wheel Qigong." Both the names Falun Gong and Falun Dafa are used to describe this practice.

geniocracy—This means "rule of the genetically fit." Rael claims to have a plan whereby this can be made a reality in a humane fashion.

glossolalia—Literally meaning "tongue speaking"; this is the technical term for the phenomenon of seeming to speak in another language while in trance or, in the case of Pentecostal worship, when baptized or speaking in the Spirit. Glossolalia can take many forms, including xenolalia, a very rare phenomenon in which the language that the entranced person is speaking can be demonstrated to be an actual language to which the individual has never been exposed.

gong (gong)—"Cultivation energy."

Highest Tantra Yoga—A complex meditation system that systematically engages all the senses (hearing, seeing, tasting, smelling), sensations, and impulses (including sexual) in a focused devotional ritual. The ritual centers on the adoration of a very powerful being, Chakrasambara or Vajrayogini. The purpose is to integrate all the parts of self together in this one focused act of adoration until one self-identifies or disappears into the meditation, becoming one with the object of worship. This is a very advanced practice, and Buddhist practitioners stress that it should be undertaken only with an experienced teacher. Most scholars trace the origin of Highest Tantra Yoga to Indian/Hindu practices.

ileke—Special beaded necklaces that are given to Orisha worshippers when they are initiated or receive their first reading. Each ileke is designed with the traditional colors and patterns of the Orisha it represents.

karma—In Falun Gong, karma is said to be a black substance that results from wrongdoing. More generally, in Hindu and Buddhist practice, karma is held to be the energy accumulated by attachment to objects and actions.

Mahayana Buddhism—This umbrella term designates all forms of Buddhism that can trace their origins to a set of scriptures called the Prajnaparamita Sutras. These scriptures started to be written about 200 to 300 years following the death of the Buddha and developed the idea of the bodhisattvas, deities who would be Buddhas. Bodhisattvas took a vow to save everyone before going on to nirvana. Most Buddhists in the world, including Tibetan Buddhists, are Mahayana Buddhists. Buddhists who rejected the Prajnaparamita Sutras and the doctrine of the bodhisattva are called Theravadin Buddhists.

millenarian—The basic notion that time/history as we know it will come to an end and a new period of great peace and harmony will be ushered in. Often there will be a period of conflict prior to the time of peace.

obi—A form of divination in Ifa. Not as important as the sixteen odu that can be performed only by a Babalawo.

odus—These are verses of divination that must be learned by heart by the Babalawo so that the great divination to Orunmila/Ifa can be conducted. This form of divination is performed using sacred cowrie shells and is only performed during very important occasions (such as life readings, major healing, or yearly readings for the community).

The Order of the Solar Temple—Also known as International Chivalric Order Solar Tradition, the Order was founded by Luc Jouret and Joseph di Mambro in 1984. Chapters of the religion are located primarily in France and Quebec, Canada. The members consider themselves to be linked to a medieval secret society, the Knights Templar. Members of the group believed that Jouret was Christ returned and that, after death, they would reincarnate on a planet orbiting the star Sirius. They also believed that the world was ending, that there was a government conspiracy to prevent them from fulfilling their mission, and that their lives had to end in fire. For several months before a series of mass suicides and murders, there were rumors that the group was suffering from financial mismanagement. Killings and suicides occurred in both French and Canadian locations over a three-year period (1994–1997) and were timed in accordance with solstices and equinoxes. Many of the deaths were not voluntary. The last incident occurred in Canada on March 20, 1997, when five adults and three teenagers attempted suicide. When the initial attempt failed, the adults allowed the teenagers to leave, and then killed themselves. In one of his final messages, Marshall Applewhite noted his approval of the suicides undertaken by members of The Solar Temple.

Orishas—Ancestral divine beings who act as mediators with the Supreme Being in the Ifa-Lukumi-Santeria-Candomble faiths. They are sometimes seen as natural forces and sometimes understood as ancestors. They are not all-powerful but are seen as natural allies of human beings. They can be considered similar to the saints or angels of other religious traditions.

qigong (chee-gong)—A general name for certain practices that cultivate the human body. In recent decades, qigong exercises have been very popular in China.

Sabbat—Any one of the eight holy days in the Wiccan calendar, such as Samhain (Halloween) or Beltane (May Day).

sadhana—Meaning "directed discipline," in Tibetan Buddhism, sadhana is a form of ritualized visualization that also serves as a devotional prayer. A disciple prays to a Buddha, bodhisattva, or dharma protector so fervently that he or she disappears into the presence of or becomes one with that being.

Santero—An individual who serves as a priest in Santeria and is roughly the equivalent of an Awo.

second baptism—This is the baptism of the Holy Spirit that follows the water baptism that earns salvation in Holiness and Pentecostal congregations. The baptism of the Holy Spirit is signaled by the special, accompanying gifts of the spirit.

Sensual Meditation—One of the principal ritual practices of the Raelian religion. It involves meditation on the organs of the body and becoming aware of the physical nature of the self. Sensual Meditation is said to increase pleasure, health, and sexual awareness. Sensual Meditation can be practiced individually or in groups.

spell—A simple ritual for magic that has a reputation for working; can be compared to a good prayer.

syncretic/syncretism—Terms describing how elements of different religious traditions can blend because of similar symbolism, ritual, or association. For example, in certain forms of Christianity, northern European elements of Spring Festivals representing the rebirth of nature—for example, eggs and rabbits—were combined with the Christian symbolism representing the resurrection of Christ. Thus, at Easter, Christ's resurrection is also celebrated with bunnies and colored eggs. In Santeria, the Orishas were associated with various Catholic saints (Chango, for example, is associated with Saint Barbara). Although this was partially done to conceal the continued worship of the Orishas, the corresponding saint was chosen because of similar symbolism, which has now become part of the worship of the Orishas.

third eye—Sometimes translated as "the Celestial Eye," this term (tianmu) is used flexibly and can refer to the Third Eye system or a particular component of that system, such as the pineal gland.

Tiananmen Square—On April 5, 1989, the largest public demonstration in recent memory occurred at this large square in Beijing, on a day traditionally set aside to honor ancestors in China. It is not known how many people actually participated in the demonstrations that continued for several weeks, but it is not unlikely that millions took their turn protesting for democratic reform of the government. On June 4, the government took decisive action and massacred hundreds of people. Many more arrests and detainments followed. The political implication of Falun Gong practitioners protesting at Tiananmen Square, the site of these events, cannot be overstated.

transmission of the cellular code—This is the Raelian baptism that involves an awakening of one's genetic memory. In this way, one can "tune" into the galactic heritage of the Elohim more effectively.

xinxing (shin-shing)—The goal of Falun Gong practice is the perfection of "mind" or "heart" nature.

yoga—Literally "to yoke," in Hinduism and Buddhism, yoga is any kind of practice that links or joins one to a devotional practice, deity, guru, or meditation goal. The practice can be physical, mental, emotional, visual, or verbal—literally, whatever works to bind a disciple to a faith or process of enlightenment. In the West, we use the word "religion" (that which binds) to denote a similar process.

Yoruba—A language and extended group of nations originally located throughout much of western Africa but now concentrated primarily in Nigeria and Benin. There are currently approximately 30 million Yoruban-speaking people in Africa. Yoruba is also the sacred language of all Ifa-Orisha faith groups.

Zhen-Shan-Ren (jhun-shahn-ren)—Truthfulness, Benevolence, and Forbearance are the three ethical principles in Falun Gong.

BIBLIOGRAPHY

Aalderink, Karin. *Totally Expunge Evil, Pursue It to the End: Explaning the Crackdown on the Falun* Gong. M.A. Thesis, Department of Chinese Studies: Leiden University, The Netherlands, 2001.

Adler, Margot. *Drawing Down the Moon: Witches, Druids, Goddess Worshippers and Other Pagans in America Today.* Revised and expanded. New York: Penguin, 1977.

Bascom, William. *Sixteen Cowries: Yoruban Divination from Africa to the New World.* Bloomington, Ind.: Indiana University Press, 1993.

Blumhofer, Edith W. *Assemblies of God: A Popular History.* Springfield, Mo.: Gospel Pub House, 1985.

Bonewits, Isaac. *Real Magic: An Introductory Treatise on the Basic Principles of Yellow Magic.* York, Maine: Weiser Books, 1989.

———. *Rites of Worship: A Neo-Pagan Approach.* Miami, Fla.: Dubsar House Publishing, 2003.

Brandon, George. *Santeria from Africa to the New World: The Dead Sell Memories.* Bloomington, Ind.: Indiana University Press, 1993.

Bromley, David G., and J. Gordon Melton, eds. *Cults, Religion, and Violence.* New York: Cambridge University Press, 2002.

Bushman, Claudia and Richard. *Building the Kingdom: A History of Mormons in America.* Oxford, U.K.: Oxford University Press, 2001.

Campbell, Barbara Anne. *Underneath This Prim Exterior: The Passion of Aimee Semple McPherson and the Construction of Public Self in Women's Ministry.* Thesis, California State University-Fullerton, 1997.

Correal, Tobe Melora. *Finding Soul on the Path of Orisa: A West African Spiritual Tradition.* New South Wales, Australia: Crossing Press, 2001.

Corten, Andre, and Ruth Marshall-Fratani. *Between Babel and Pentecost: Transnational Pentecostalism in Africa and Latin America.* Bloomington, Ind.: Indiana University Press, 2001.

Cortez, Julio Garcia. *The Osha: Secrets of the Yoruba-Lucumi-Santeria Religion in the United States and the Americas.* Brooklyn, N.Y.: Athelia Henrietta Press, 2000.

Cox, Harvey. *Fire from Heaven: The Rise of Pentecostal Spirituality and the Reshaping of Religion in the 21st Century.* Cambridge, Mass.: Da Capo Press, 2001.

Cunningham, Scott. *Wicca: A Guide for the Solitary Practitioner.* St. Paul, Minn.: Llewellyn Publications, 1988.

Dreyfus, Georges. "The Shuk-den Affair: Origins of a Controversy." Williams College, 1999. Address found at http://www.tibet.com/dholgyal/shugden-origins.html.

Dupree, Sherry Sherrod. *African-American Holiness Pentecostal Movement: An Annotated Bibliography.* New York: Garland Publishing, 1995.

Edwards, Paul M. *Our Legacy of Faith: A Brief History of the Reorganized Church of Jesus Christ of Latter Day Saints.* Independence, Mo.: Herald Publishing House, 1991.

Ellwood, Robert A. "UFO Religious Movements," in *America's Alternative Religions.* Edited by Timothy Miller. Albany, N.Y.: SUNY Press, 1995.

Epstein, Daniel Mark. *Sister Aimee.* New York: Harcourt, Brace, Jovanovich, 1993.

Farrar, Janet and Stewart. *A Witch's Bible: The Complete Witch's Handbook.* Tipperary, Republic of Ireland: Phoenix Publishing, 1996.

Fatumbi, Awo Fa'Lokun. *Awo: Ifa and the Theology of Orisha Divination.* New York: Original Publications, 1992.

Givens, Terryl L. *By the Hand of Mormon: The American Scripture That Launched a New World Religion.* Oxford, U.K.: Oxford University Press, 2002.

Gyatso, Geshe Kelsang. *Heart Jewel: The Essential Practices of Kadampa Buddhism.* Glen Spey, N.Y.: Tharpa Publications, 1997.

BIBLIOGRAPHY

A Handbook of Tibetan Culture: A Guide to Tibetan Centres and Resources throughout the World. Compiled by Orient Foundation, edited by Graham Coleman. Boston, Mass.: Shambhala Press, 1994.

Hayford, Jack. *A New Time and Place.* Sisters, Ore: Multnomah, 1997.

Hutton, Ronald. *Triumph of the Moon: A History of Modern Pagan Witchcraft.* Oxford, U.K.: Oxford University Press, 2001.

Karade, Baba Ife. *The Handbook of Yoruba Religious Concepts.* York, Maine: Weiser Books, 1994.

Kay, David. "The New Kadampa Tradition and the Continuity of Tibetan Buddhism in Transition," *Journal of Contemporary Religion* 12:3 (October 1997), 277–293.

Lopez, David S. Jr. *Prisoners of Shangri-La: Tibetan Buddhism and the West.* Chicago, Ill.: University of Chicago Press, 1998.

Luhrman, T.M. *Persuasions of the Witch's Craft: Ritual Magic in Contemporary England.* Cambridge, Mass.: Harvard University Press, 1991.

McClung, L. Grant Jr. *Azusa Street and Beyond: Pentecostal Missions and Church Growth in the Twentieth Century.* Los Angeles, Calif.: Bridge Publications, 1986.

Melton, J. Gordon. *Magic, Witchcraft and Paganism in America.* New York: Garland Publishing, 1992.

———, and Martin Baumann, eds. *Religions of the World: A Comprehensive Encyclopedia of Beliefs and Practices.* Santa Barbara, Calif.: ABC-CLIO, 2002.

Miller, Timothy, ed. *America's Alternative Religions.* Albany, N.Y.: SUNY Press, 1995.

Murphy, Joseph M., and Mei Mei Sanford. *Osun across the Waters: A Yoruba Goddess in Africa and the Americas.* Bloomington, Ind.: Indiana University Press, 2001.

Neimark, Philip. *The Way of the Orisa: Empowering Your Life through the Ancient African Religion of Ifa.* San Francisco, Calif.: HarperSanFrancisco, 1993.

Newman, Bruce. *A Beginner's Guide to Tibetan Buddhism: Notes from a Practitioner's Journey.* Ithaca, N.Y.: Snow Lion Publications, 2004.

Palmer, Susan Jean. "Women in the Raelian Movement: New Religious Experiments in Gender and Authority," in *The Gods Have Landed: New Religions from Other Worlds.* Edited by James R. Lewis. Albany, N.Y.: SUNY Press, 1995.

Rael, Claude. *The Final Message.* Norwich, U.K.: The Tagman Press, 1998.

Remini, Robert Vincent. *Joseph Smith.* New York: Viking Press, 2002.

Shields, Steven L. "The Latter Day Saint Churches" in *America's Alternative Religions.* Albany, N.Y.: SUNY Press, 1995.

Sopa, Geshe, and Jeffrey Hopkins. *Cutting through Appearances: Practice and Theory of Tibetan Buddhism.* Ithaca, N.Y.: Snow Lion Publications, 1989.

Starhawk. *The Spiral Dance, 20-Year Anniversary Edition: A Rebirth of the Ancient Religion of the Goddess.* San Francisco, Calif.: HarperSanFrancisco, 1999.

Synan, Vinson. *The Holiness-Pentecostal Tradition: Charismatic Movements in the Twentieth Century.* Grand Rapids, Mich.: Wm. B. Eerdmans, 1997.

Teish, Luisah. *Jambalaya: The Natural Woman's Book of Personal Charms and Practical Rituals.* San Francisco, Calif.: HarperSanFrancisco, 1988.

Ter Haar, Barend. *Falun Gong: Evaluation and Further References.* Leiden University, The Netherlands, 2002.

Thompson, Robert Farris. *Flash of the Spirit: African and Afro-American Art and Philosophy.* New York: Random House, 1983.

Thorsson, Edred. *At the Well of Wyrd: A Handbook of Runic Divination.* York, Maine: Red Wheel/Weiser, 1988.

BIBLIOGRAPHY

Thurman, Robert A.F. *The Central Philosophy of Tibet.* Princeton, N.J.: Princeton University Press, 1991.

Tricycle: The Buddhist Review, Vol. VII, No. 3 (Spring 1998).

Voeks, Robert. *Sacred Leaves of Candomble.* Austin, Tex.: University of Texas Press, 1997.

Vorilhon, Claude. *Extraterrestrials Took Me to Their Planet.* Brantome, France: l'Edition du Message, 1986.

———. *Sensual Meditation: Awakening the Mind by Awakening the Body.* Tokyo: AOM Corp., 1978.

Wacker, Grant. *Heaven Below: Early Pentecostals and American Culture.* Cambridge, Mass.: Harvard University Press, 2003.

Weinstein, Marion. *Positive Magic: Ancient Metaphysical Techniques for Modern Lives.* Franklin Lakes, N.J.: New Page Books, 2002.

Wong, John, and William T. Liu. *The Mystery of China's Falun Gong: Its Rise and Its Sociological Implications.* National University of Singapore: East Asian Institute, 1999.

Chen, Nancy N. *Breathing Spaces: Qigong, Psychiatry, and Healing in China.* New York: Columbia University Press, 2003.

Guest, Kenneth J. *God in Chinatown: Religion and Survival in New York's Evolving Immigrant Community.* New York: New York University Press, 2003.

Kisaka, Robert J., and Mark Mullins. *Religion and Social Crisis in Japan: Understanding Japanese Society through the Aum Affair.* New York: Palgrave, 1998.

Lewis, James R. *Controversial New Religions.* New York: Oxford University Press, 2004.

———. *Legitimating New Religions.* New Brunswick, N.J.: Rutgers University Press, 2003.

———. *The Oxford Handbook of New Religious Movements.* New York: Oxford University Press, 2004.

Lifton, Robert Jay. *Destroying the World to Save It: Aum Shinrikyo: Apocalyptic Violence and New Global Terrorism.* New York: Metropolitan Books, 1999.

Palmer, Susan J. *Aliens Adored: Rael's UFO Religion.* New Brunswick, N.J.: Rutgers University Press, 2004.

Partridge, Christopher. *UFO Religion.* London: Routledge, 2003.

Porter, Noah, *Falun Gong in the United States: An Ethnographic Study.* Dissertation.com, 2003.

Seiwert, Hubert (in collaboration with Ma Xisha). *Popular Religious Movements and Heterodox Sects in Chinese History.* Boston, Mass.: Brill, 2003.

Thompson, Leonard. *The Book of Revelation: Apocalypse and Empire.* New York: Oxford University Press, 1990.

Wessinger, Catherine. *How the Millennium Comes Violently: From Jonestown to Heaven's Gate.* New York: Seven Bridges Books, 2000.

WEBSITES

Official Site of Church of Jesus Christ of Latter-day Saints
www.lds.org

Official Site of the LDS Church in the United Kingdom
http://www.lds.org.uk/

LDS Information
http://www.mormon.org/

Official Community of Christ (Independence, Missouri)
http://www.cofchrist.org/

Community of Christ (Australia)
http://www.saintschurch.org.au/

Official Site of Church of Christ (Temple Lot, Independence, Missouri)
http://www.churchofchrist-tl.org/

Official Site of International Baha'i Movement
http://www.bahai.org

Official Site of Baha'is of the United States
http://www.us.bahai.org/

The Online Newsletter of the International Baha'i Community
http://www.onecountry.org/

Baha'i Educational Site for Children in the United States
http://www.education.usbnc.org/

Official Site of the Orthodox Baha'i Faith
http://www.rt66.com/~obfusa/council.htm

Official Site of the International Foursquare Church
http://www.foursquare.org/

Site of a Well-Known Foursquare Congregation
http://www.libertyharbor.org/index.html

Site of a "Seed" Church in Lawrence, Kansas
http://www.faithfoursquare.com

Official Site of the International Raelian Movement
http://www.rael.org/

Newspaper Articles about Raelians
http://www.rickross.com/groups/raelians.html

Online Magazine on Raelian Information
http://www.subversions.com/

Official Clonaid Site
http://www.clonaid.com/news.php

Official Site of the Raelian UFO Theme Park, UFOland
http://www.ufoland.com/building/english/pages/build.html

Site that Explores and Advocates Geniocracy
http://www.geniocracy.net/index.htm

Philip Neimark's Website
http://www.ifafoundation.org/

Site of the Hialeah, Florida Lukumi Church
http://www.church-of-the-lukumi.org/index.html

Site for the Kingdom of Oyotunji, South Carolina
http://www.cultural-expressions.com/oyotunji/default.htm

Traditional Orisha Chants
http://batadrums.bigstep.com/

University of Wisconsin Site about Learning the Yoruban Language
http://african.lss.wisc.edu/yoruba/index.html

Traditional Site Located in Florida with Links to Nigeria
http://www.ifainc.org/main/navigation.html

Information on How to Study for the Priesthood (Awo)
http://www.awostudycenter.com/

Sites Providing Information about Santeria in Cuba
http://www.mojomoon.net/santeria.html#orishas
http://www.ipfw.edu/mfl/cuba/Santeria/orishas.htm

WEBSITES

Site about Candomble and Orisha
http://fullmoon_deities.tripod.com/candomble.html

Site about Candomble
http://candomble.davidtalbot.net/

International Introduction to Falun Gong/Falun Dafa
http://www.falundafa.org/

Li Hongzhi's Texts
http://www.falundafa.org/book/eng/flg.htm

Falun Gong's Political Activity
http://www.faluninfo.net/

Official American Falun Gong Site
http://www.fofg.org/

Article Written in Defense of Wiccans
http://www.wicca.com/celtic/wicca/christian.htm

Article Written by a Christian Working in an Australian Wiccan Church
http://www.shootthemessenger.com.au/u_jun_99/i_wicca.htm

Official Site of Circle Sanctuary
http://www.circlesanctuary.org/

Official Church of All Worlds Site
http://www.caw.org/

Official Church of Wicca Site
http://wicca.org/

Homepage of Janet Frost and Gavin Bone (Wiccans)
http://www.wicca.utvinternet.com/

Homepage of the Kansas City Heartland Spiritual Alliance
http://www.kchsa.org/

Homepage of the Asatru Free Assembly
http://www.runestone.org/flash/introduction/index.html

Article on Neo-Paganism
http://www.newdawnmagazine.com/articles/Conversation%20wit
h%20Dr%20Stephen%20Flowers.html

New Religious Movements on an International Scale
www.cesnur.org

Site for Mainstream and Marginal Religious Groups
www.religioustolerance.org

Religious Movements Site
http://religiousmovements.lib.virginia.edu

International New Kadampa Site
http://www.kadampa.org/english/index.php

**BBC (British Broadcasting Corporation) Feature about New
Kadampa Tradition**
http://www.bbc.co.uk/religion/religions/buddhism/
features/kadampa/

New Kadampa Teachings for Children and Their Parents
http://www.rameshori.com/classes_family.html

Information about Dorje Shugden Controversy
http://www.cesnur.org/testi/NKT.htm

Site Dedicated to Dorje Shugden
http://www.shugden.com/

**Tibetan Government in Exile Site Regarding the Worship
of Dorje Shugden**
http://www.tibet.com/dholgyal/

Anticultist Sites
http://www.rickross.com/
http://www.peopleunitedforreligiousfreedom.org/
http://www.scp-inc.org/
http://www.watchman.org/
http://www.newcovpub.com/

INDEX

Aaron, 15
Aaronic priesthood, 25, 27, 30
ABC's of Witchcraft, 115
Abdu'l-Baha, 38–39, 40, 47
Abdu'l-Baha's Ascension, 43
abortion
    and Church of Jesus Christ of
      Latter-day Saints, 32
    and Raelians, 71, 74
ache (ashe), 80
Adamski, George, 63
Adefunmi, Oseijeman, 91
Adler, Margo, 115
Aetherius Society, 63
Africa
    and Ifa, 10, 78, 79, 80, 81, 84–85,
      86–87, 90, 90–91, 92, 93–94.
      See also Orisha worship
    and Neo-Paganism, 111
    and Quimbanda, 79
    and Umbanda, 79
    and Vodu, 79, 92
African American Churches, and
    Pentecostal-charismatic worship
    style, 60–61
African Americans
    and Baha'i faith, 44
    and Church of Jesus Christ of
      Latter-day Saints, 32
    and Foursquare Gospel Church,
      54, 60
    and Orisha worship, 91
    and Pentecostalism, 53, 60.
    See also racism
African Methodist Episcopal
    Church, and Pentecostal-charismatic
    worship style, 60–61
African Theological Archministry,
    Inc., 91
afterlife, and Church of Jesus Christ
    of Latter-day Saints, 22, 23
alcohol
    and Baha'i faith, 42
    and Church of Jesus Christ of
      Latter-day Saints, 27

Aleph, 149.
    See also Aum Shinri Kyo
Alexanderian Wicca, 114, 117.
    See also Wicca
Ali, Husayn, 37.
    See also Baha'u'llah
aliens
    and Falun Gong, 101, 103, 104,
      106
    and Human Individual Meta-
      morphosis, 150
Ali Muhammad. *See* Bab, The
Aluko, Chief, 85
Amber K, 115
American Ifa, 84–85
American Wicca, 114
ancient worship, and Neo-Paganism/
    Wicca, 111, 113
Andrews, Ted, 115
Angelus Temple, 55, 58
Anglo-Saxons, and Wicca, 111,
    120–121
animal sacrifice, and Orisha worship,
    79, 84, 84–85, 87, 91–93
animals, and Orisha worship, 80,
    81
Animator, 68
Annwfn, 120
anthropology, and Neo-Paganism,
    113
anticultists, 147, 153, 154
Apostles. *See* Quorum of Twelve
Apostolic Congress, 52
Applewhite, Marshall ("Do,"
    "The Present Representative"),
    150–151, 154
appointees, and Foursquare Gospel
    Church, 56
archaeology, and Neo-Paganism,
    113
Area Authorites, 25
areas, and Church of Jesus Christ
    of Latter-day Saints, 25
Articles of Faith, The, 21
Asahara, Shoko, 148, 149, 154

INDEX

INDEX

INDEX

INDEX

Millerites, The, 9.
  See also Seventh-day Adventists, The
missions
  and Church of Jesus Christ of
    Latter-day Saints, 27–28
  and Foursquare Gospel Church,
    56, 58, 59
  and Pentecostalism, 55
Missoula, Montana, and Baha'i
  Under the Provisions of the
  Covenant, 48
Missouri
  and Church of Jesus Christ of
    Latter-day Saints, 15, 23
  and Community of Christ, 17
  and Neo-Paganism/Wicca, 125
Montana, and Baha'i Under the
  Provisions of the Covenant, 48
Montreal, Canada, and Raelians,
  71, 73
morality, and Falun Gong, 99, 100,
  102
Mormon, 18
Mormon Tabernacle Choir, 28–29
Mormons. *See* Church of Jesus
  Christ of Latter-day Saints
Moroni, 14
Morrill Anti-Bigamy Law of 1862, 31
Moses, 67
Most Holy Book, The, 38
Mother Baha'i Council, 48
Mount Carmel, and Branch Davidians,
  145–147, 152, 153, 154
Mountain Meadow Massacre, 31,
  156
movement, 6
Muhammad, 7, 67, 67.
  See also Islam
music
  and Baha'i faith, 44–45
  and Church of Jesus Christ of
    Latter-day Saints, 28–29
  and Foursquare Gospel Church,
    57
  and Orisha worship, 84, 89

mythologies
  and Neo-Paganism, 111, 114
  and Wicca, 111, 114

naming, and Orisha worship,
  90
National Church Division, 56
National Spiritual Assemblies, 41,
  44, 47, 48
Native Americans. *See*
  Indians/Native Americans
natural forces, and Orisha worship,
  80, 81
nature
  and Neo-Paganism/Wicca, 111,
    113, 115–116, 127
Nauvoo, Illinois, and Church of
  Jesus Christ of Latter-day Saints,
  16, 17
Naw Ruz, 41, 42, 45
Nemeton, 120
Neo-Paganism, 6, 11, 110–127
  and controversies, 125–127
  and family and children,
    124–125
  and foundations, 111, 113, 114,
    127
  and growing up, 124–125
  and holidays and ceremonies,
    121–124
  and magic, 116–117, 121–124,
    125
  and members, 111, 114, 119
  and organization, 117, 119–120
  and scriptures, 114–115,
    124–125
  Wicca *versus*, 111
  and witchcraft, 111, 114, 125
  in world today, 127
  and worldview, 115–117.
  See also Wicca
Nephi/Nephites, 18, 19
Nest, 120
Nettles, Bonnie Lu Trusdale
  ("Ti"), 150

INDEX

PICTURE CREDITS

Page:

B: © Joseph Sohm; ChromoSohm Inc./
CORBIS
C: © Richard T. Nowitz/CORBIS
D: (top) © Bettmann/CORBIS
D: (bottom) © Getty Images

E: © Dennis di Cicco/CORBIS
F: © Werner Forman/Art Resource, NY
G: © AFP/Getty Images
H: © REBECCA MCETEE/
CORBIS SYGMA

Cover: © Richard Cummins/CORBIS
Frontis: Associated Press Graphics

CONTRIBUTORS

CAROL S. MATTHEWS has been interested in New Religious Movements all her life. She graduated from the University of Kansas with an M.A. in Religious Studies and a Ph.D. in American Studies. Her specialties are Race and Religious Cultures and the History of New Religious Movements in the United States. Recently, she was awarded a Kluge Fellowship from the Library of Congress. She currently teaches American History and Comparative Religion classes in the Kansas City, Missouri, area where she resides with many books and four very healthy cats. She is proud to count practitioners of every single religion mentioned in this book (and more) as her friends and associates.

ANN MARIE B. BAHR is professor of religious studies at South Dakota State University. Her areas of teaching, research, and writing include World Religions, New Testament, Religion in American Culture, and the Middle East. Her articles have appeared in *Annual Editions: World Religions 03/04* (Guilford, Conn.: McGraw-Hill, 2003), *The Journal of Ecumenical Studies*, and *Covenant for a New Creation: Ethics, Religion and Public Policy* (Maryknoll, N.Y.: Orbis, 1991). Since 1999, she has authored a weekly newspaper column which analyzes the cultural significance of religious holidays. She has served as president of the Upper Midwest Region of the American Academy of Religion.

MARTIN E. MARTY, an ordained minister in the Evangelical Lutheran Church in America, is the Fairfax M. Cone Distinguished Service Professor Emeritus at the University of Chicago Divinity School, where he taught for thirty-five years. Marty has served as president of the American Academy of Religion, the American Society of Church History, and the American Catholic Historical Association, and was also a member of two U.S. presidential commissions. He is currently Senior Regent at St. Olaf College in Northfield, Minnesota. Marty has written more than fifty books, including the three-volume *Modern American Religion* (University of Chicago Press). His book *Righteous Empire* was a recipient of the National Book Award.